THROUGH THE BATTLES WITHOUT THE SCARS

Keys to Understanding and Living Life Successfully

BERTRAM SMITH

Through the Battles without the Scars: Keys to Understanding and Living Life Successfully
Copyright © 2024 Bertram Smith

All rights reserved.

No part of this book may be reproduced, stored, or transmitted by any means—whether auditory, graphic, mechanical, or electronic—without written permission of both publisher and author, except in the case of brief excerpts used in critical articles and reviews. Unauthorized reproduction of any part of this work is illegal and is punishable by law.

Scripture quotations are taken from the *Holy Bible*, New Living Translation, copyright ©1996, 2004, 2015 by Tyndale House Foundation. Used by permission of Tyndale House Publishers, Carol Stream, Illinois 60188. All rights reserved.

Cover Art by Patrick Noze
www.patricknoze.com

Cover Design and Interior Formatting by Jose Pepito
Inspire Books
www.inspire-books.com

Published by Impel Books
https://www.bookstoinspireus.com/

Print ISBN: 979-8-9911908-0-0
Ebook ISBN: 979-8-9911908-1-7
Printed in the United States

We say that life is a journey
And yes, that is true
Partially
For even as a journey
Life
This life
The life we live
Ever since the Fall of Humanity
Has been a battle
So
A more complete and summative picture
And understanding of life
Is that
Even as a journey…
Life still becomes a battle!

Then Joseph brought in his father, Jacob, and presented him to Pharaoh. And Jacob blessed Pharaoh.

"How old are you?" Pharaoh asked him.

Jacob replied, "I have traveled this earth for 130 hard years. But my life has been short compared to the lives of my ancestors."

—Genesis 47:7-9, emphasis mine

When Pharaoh finally let the people go, God did not lead them along the main road that runs through Philistine territory, even though that was the shortest route to the Promised Land. God said, "If the people are faced with a battle (this soon), they might change their minds and return to Egypt." Thus the Israelites left Egypt like an army ready for battle.

—Exodus 13:17-22, emphasis and parenthetical mine

Contents

Keys to Understanding Life—and This Book ix
Preface xiii
Life Was Not Always a Battle xv
Introduction
Chapter 1 1
Chapter 2 18
Chapter 3 31
Chapter 4 54
Chapter 5 71
Chapter 6 85
Chapter 7 100
Chapter 8 112
Chapter 9 131
Chapter 10 177
Chapter 11 201
Chapter 12 216
Chapter 13 237
Chapter 14 251
About the Author 277
About the Illustrator 279

Keys to Understanding Life— and This Book

1. Life is a battle.
2. As a battle, life produces, manufactures, and spawns other battles.
3. All battles are spiritual in nature.
4. Battles produce wounds.
5. Wounds can and do turn into scars.
6. Scars are the long-term wounds we suffer in life as a result of our battles.
7. Scars are the wounds that won't heal.
8. The scars are the wounds produced in us that *we* allow to not heal.
9. God has given us a measure of control over our lives.
10. Thus, we have control over our wounds and can prevent them from turning into scars.
11. The scars are dangerous.
12. The scars can be deadly.
13. God uses our battles—and our wounds—to test us, prove us.
14. We live our lives at the intersection of our battles and our wounds.

Jesus showed us

The goal of life is to go through the battle—and the battles—without incurring any of the scars

> I have told you all this so that you may have peace in me. Here on earth you will have many trials and sorrows. But take heart, because I have overcome the world (John 16:33).

The scars are on us

That is to say that we are responsible for our wounds turning, or not turning, into scars

To be clear

The scars are wounds

The scars are those wounds that won't heal

They grow and fester

The scars are those wounds that won't heal precisely because we refuse to allow them to heal

Now, it is true that our wounds/scars may stem from our perception that someone has done us wrong

Hurt us

Done us an injustice or string of injustices

Or have abused us

Oftentimes

What we may perceive as a wound is not the actual wound at all

It is just part of the battle—life

Life can be harsh

We should never make light of it

Life happens to all of us

The real wounds are what are produced in us from going through the battle—and the battles

Oftentimes

The real wounds come as a reaction to what we ourselves perceive as a wound

The real wounds are such debilitating things such as

Anger

Hatred

Bitterness

Resentment

Jealousy

Unforgiveness

Pride

Covetousness

And the like

These are the things that can really harm us, lead to our spiritual demise

Preface

The first thing we need to come to know, understand, appreciate, and accept about life is that life is a battle

This is no cliché

It is not just some old, worn-out cliché about life

This statement is beyond cliché in every sense of the word

A cliché

Something we say nonchalantly

In passing

And with little thought

Something that can belie the truth

Nor is this statement concerning life just a metaphor

A metaphor for life

We are not merely comparing life to a battle

To say it again

Life itself is a battle!

This is perhaps the most simple yet profound statement that we can make concerning life

As a matter of fact, from the moment we enter life, we enter a battle

Life truly is a battle

Life Was Not Always a Battle

Life was not always, nor was it ever intended to be a battle
A struggle
Life was not meant to be plagued with difficulties
Something to be grappled with
Life was never meant to be as daunting as it is
Challenging
Or overpowering
Life was never meant to be filled with all of the struggles
Toil
Trials
Tribulations
Challenges
Sicknesses
Diseases
Demons and demon-possessions
Dying
Death
Sorrows
Troubles
Tests or temptations

All the struggles and challenges we see and have today
These are all related to what life has become
In other words, life was not meant to be a battle
It got turned into one

Introduction

The Nature of the Battle—and the Battles—we Face

Life is a battle
Plain and simple
We face—or we will face—many battles in our lifetime
These battles all stem from the battle we call life
The battle that is life

As a battle, life produces, manufactures, and spawns its own set of battles
These battles are produced by life
Not in spite of life, not in addition to life, but because of life

The battles we face are many
Just to name a few
There are physical battles
Spiritual battles
Battles related to our health
We battle emotionally
Mentally
Psychologically

There are battles that are both emotional and psychological

Some of us wrestle with health issues

Sometimes, these health issues and challenges are most serious and challenging

Spurning yet other battles

For example, we may battle high blood pressure

Or hypertension

Diabetes

Heart-related problems

Heart disease

Cancer

We experience back pains

Shoulder pain

Hip pains

Pain in our joints

Arthritis

We battle blindness

Deafness

Or the ability to walk

These are just some of the battles we face in life

Then there are the financial challenges and struggles

Challenges related to our families

Family-related issues and crises

There are marital issues

The battle to remain faithful

Faithful to God
Faithful to our spouses and our children
Some of us may be contemplating marriage break-ups
Going through a painful divorce
Something that affects the entire family
Especially children
Some of us are having to deal with unruly children
These battles are all produced in and by life
As long as we are alive, we will go through them
Something as simple as the common cold, a flu, or a toothache, can be a battle

Some of us have a difficult time controlling our eating
We have all kinds of eating disorders
We battle to lose weight
Eat right
We may be going through battles on our jobs
In our churches
Jockeying for positions and titles
To get our voices heard
Clamoring for promotions
We battle joblessness
We battle all different types of conflicts
We battle the question of whether to love and forgive
We can be battling some form of addiction
A drug addiction

Alcohol

Some of us are addicted to food

The wrong kinds of food

Food that can kill us prematurely

Then we blame it on God

Some of us may have a sex addiction

One of the greatest areas of battle and struggle is in the area of self-control

Then there are the battles that are all too real

Some of us right now are locked in legal wranglings

Battling homelessness

Not having a place to stay

Living in shelters

Out on the street

Under a bridge

We also have battles related to our faith

We may waver and falter faith-wise

Some of us, from time to time, may go through a crisis of faith

This can take place at the individual level

Or on any level

The world we live in—right now—is suffering from a crisis of faith

Faith, or trust, in our leaders

Our civic and religious leaders

Faith in our political, economic, as well as our social system
Faith
A lack of faith
A crisis of faith, I submit to you, is the greatest battle and challenge of our time
Of all times
That is, once life was turned into a battle
We battle fear

Anxiety
The feeling of loneliness
depression
A sense of inadequacy
Self-confidence or self-esteem
Some of us have an identity crises
We don't know who we are
These are only some of the challenges, battles, we face in life
Produced by life
These challenges and battles come from Just being alive
In life
On this earth
Again, these are only some of the battles we face
We are constantly battling something

All Battles Are Spiritual

We must know and understand that all battles are spiritual

Spiritual

It is not a word that is as deep as it sounds

It simply means having a physical as well as a spirit component

We are part of this earthly world as well as the spirit realm

What happens in one affects the other

They are connected

As a matter of fact, we ourselves are made from both physical matter and what is spirit

Thus

We are spiritual

Whether we are prepared to believe and accept it or not, this is true

Our battles are more spiritual than we may think

That is to say, connected to the spirit realm

What is happening "out there"

All battles are spiritual

They are connected, conditioned by, and reflect what is happening in the spirit world

Our real enemies are not humans

As a matter of fact, they are not at all

They are human only in the sense that humans are who we interface with

And

We humans allow ourselves to be used by the enemy

The enemy is Satan

The devil

We can choose to believe it or not, but the devil is real

This

The spiritual nature of life

Is what prompted the apostle Paul to write:

> For we are not fighting against flesh-and-blood enemies, but against evil rulers and authorities of the unseen world, against mighty powers in this dark world, and against evil spirits in the heavenly places (Eph 6:12).

In other words, what the apostle Paul is saying is that battles have a spiritual component to them

Our real battles are not with human beings (flesh-and-blood)

Battles can be deeply spiritual

Intense

We will all go through many battles in our lifetime

Battles Produce Other Battles

Not only is life a battle, but Life also produces, manufactures, and spawns other battles

This is the nature of life

Indeed, there are battles that stem from our battles

Yes, the array of battles we face stems from the battle we are in

Life!

The battles we just mentioned, they all come from simply being alive

They stem from life

The fact that we are here on planet earth

There Are Battles—And Signs of Battles—All Around Us

There is a battle at the center of life

We ourselves are at the center of an intense battle or struggle

This is the battle being waged for the human soul

Our soul is essentially us

We are tri-layered

Physical, spirit, and then soul

Our spirit houses our souls

This is why Jesus said

> Don't be afraid of those who want to kill your body; they cannot touch your soul. Fear only God, who can destroy both soul and body in hell (Matthew 10:28).

There is also a battle raging on the inside of us

A battle that spells the absence or the "deactivation" of God in our lives

There are battles that we can see and battles we cannot see

Let me implore you to read on your own 2 Kings 17–20

Instinctively—we know life to be a battle

Yes

Deep down in our spirits, we know life to be a battle

We know it consciously and subconsciously—even unconsciously

It comes across in the way we speak

Talk about life

In our daily parlance about life

Talk to someone

Ask them how they are doing, and you will probably get one of these eerily subconscious/unconscious responses

"It's tough, man!"

"It's rough!"

"Man, it's a battle out there!"

"I am right here catching hell!"

"Just holding on"

"Trying to hold on"

How about this one?

"Right here, trying to keep my head above water"

Or this one

"It's a struggle, man, it's a struggle!"

I like this one

"The struggle continues!"

Note: All of these are fighting words

Dueling words

Words that tell of a war

We even call it spiritual warfare

All words that point to life as a battle

Now, these are not great responses to life or about life

However, they do reflect a certain reality of what we all know deep down inside

I was in the food store the other day

In the checkout line

I couldn't help but notice that the young lady, who happened to be the cashier, was not smiling

As a matter of fact, she was pretty stone-faced, stoic, and glum

Talk about doing one's job vacuously

She was ignoring the customers

Mechanically sliding the items down the conveyor belt and uncaringly handing the customers their receipts

No "thank you," "bye-bye," or anything of that sort

When it was my turn, I decided to speak to her

Maybe cheer her up a little

"Hi! How are you doing?" I said

I was not prepared for her response

It caught me completely off guard

Almost floored me

She did not even look up

But I will never forget her words

She said

"Black, broke, and depressed!"

To say that I was caught off guard would be an understatement

I was shocked

Stunned

Comeback?

I had none!

What was I to say to that?

How was I to respond?

When I finally regained my composure—and my words—all I could say was:

"Well, I hope you feel better soon."

We are all going through something

Sometimes, what we are going through will register on our faces

Sometimes, it does not

Sometimes, it just comes tumbling out

Cain, in the Bible, was going through an intense internal struggle

God said to Cain:

> "Why are you so angry?" the LORD asked Cain. "Why do you look so dejected?" (Genesis 4:6).

Cain, because of what he was battling, looked "dejected!"

Life truly is a battle
On every level
On every front
In every way

Of course, this is not to say that we are to be depressed in and by life
There is joy in life
Much joy!
In the midst of the battle, we celebrate
However, we must understand that life is a "dress rehearsal" for the next life
The best way to view life is as potentially short-term pain for long-term pleasure
So life is worth celebrating
Indeed, we celebrate as we go through the battles

CHAPTER 1

Battles Are Known by Many Names

We refer to battles as many things

By many names

We sometimes refer to battles as

Yes—battles, of course!

But we also refer to them as

Wars

Fires

Storms

Winds

Headwinds

Trials

Tests

Difficulties

Tribulations

Oppositions

Persecution

Troubles

Struggles

Trials

Sorrows

And more

Jesus said:

"Here on earth you will have many **trials** and **sorrows**. But take heart, because I have overcome the world" (John 16:33, emphasis mine).

So Jesus offers us a caveat

A reassurance:

> "But take heart, because I have overcome the world."

Jesus was saying

Affirming

First

That life is a battle

But

Secondly

We can

It is possible

With God's help

To go through the battle that is life—and the battles spurned by life

Why?

Because Jesus

God

In all of His humanity as He walked this Earth

Experiencing the full range of human trials

Physical limitations

Emotions

And temptations

He did!

He went through the battles

The storms

And the fires

Dealt with life

Had to put up with life

As a human being

Just like we do!

One of the attendant reasons for Jesus' coming was to model for us how to go through the battle—and the battles!

Jesus also says in Matthew 28:29:

I am with you always, even to the end of the age.

How?

Through the presence of the Holy Spirit!

God said in Isaiah 41:10:

> Don't be discouraged, for I am your God. I will strengthen you and help you. I will hold you up with my victorious right hand.

Again

Jesus said in John 17:13-15

(Praying to the Father to protect His disciples as they go through the battle)

> Now I am coming to you. I told them many things while I was with them in this world so they would be filled with my joy. I have given them your word. And the world hates them because they do not belong to the world, just as I do not belong to the world. I'm not asking you to take them out of the world, but to keep them safe from the evil one (emphasis mine).

The world

People of the world

And Satan

And his demons

These are all what is meant by "the world"

As far as people are concerned

Those who don't know and are not willing to accept the truth

Who are kept locked

Blinded

Imprisoned in darkness by the enemy's lies

The lies of the devil

Satan

All those who fight against Truth

The Bible says that this world is ruled and controlled by the evil one

Satan

The devil, temptations are a part of this life—the battle—and the battles we face

Jesus knew that because His disciples belonged to Him

And they would be responsible for sharing the truth about Him, that they would have yet another layer of battles added to the normal battles and challenges we face

(The Gospel of Jesus Christ, sadly, attracts opposition like how flies are attracted to light!)

For God's people

Those of us who would dare to speak truth

Share Truth

The battle—and the battles—become even more intense

But speaking of joy in and in the midst of our battles

Jesus said in Matthew 5:11-12:

> God blesses you when people mock you and persecute you and lie about you and say all sorts of evil things against you because you are my followers. Be happy about it! Be very glad! For a great reward awaits you in heaven. And remember, the ancient prophets were persecuted in the same way.

Wait!

Did Jesus really say

We are blessed when mocked, persecuted, lied upon, and have all sorts of evil things said about us simply because we follow Him, belong to Him?

Did He really say we should be happy about it?

Exceedingly glad?

That there is a reward?

A reward for going through the battle?

Suffering the slings and arrows of this life?

Yes, He did!

We have to understand that what happens to us in this life are not the real wounds

We tend to think of them as real wounds

We perceive them as wounds

The evils

The injustices

The wrongs

Injuries

Abuses

When, in actual fact, they are life

Just life

Simply reflective of what life has been turned into

What life has become

Just part of the battle

Life, sadly, happens to all of us

The key is how we respond to life

How we respond to the wrongs
The hurts
The pains
The injustices
The evil treatment
The mistreatment
The abuses
No, they are not wounds at all
We perceive them as wounds!
However, they are more like tests
Opportunities
Opportunities to be blessed by God

> Dear brothers and sisters, when troubles of any kind come your way, consider it an opportunity for great joy. For you know that when your faith is tested, your endurance has a chance to grow. So let it grow, for when your endurance is fully developed, you will be perfect and complete, needing nothing (James 1:2-4).

The "stuff" that happens to us in life
Depending on how we react to them
Is what really produces in us the wounds
The real wounds
The real wounds of this life
The wounds that are sin
They come from within
They are produced in us

Yes

Life is a battle

Battles produce all kinds of other battles

Our battles are spiritual

These battles

Depending on how we respond to them

produce the wounds

The real wounds

The unfortunate sins in our lives

This is because the wounds are sins

The real wounds come from how we respond to the battle—and the battles

How we respond to what happens to us

How we respond to what others do to us

The real wounds come as a result of how we respond to what happens to us

These are the real wounds that can lead to even deeper wounds

Deeper wounds we call scars

The wounds that can lead to our spiritual and permanent deaths

For those who know God

And are called according to His purpose

God is in control

How are we to respond to what happens to us in life?

The battles
The injustices
We are not supposed to
We are not to take matters into our own hands
Not react
Not over-react
Not react at all
If anything, we are to do the unexpected
The complete opposite
Shower our enemies with love
This is not easy
in fact it can be painfully difficult
However, this is how God has designed life to work
God is all wisdom!
Paul says:

> Instead, "If your enemies are hungry, feed them. If they are thirsty, give them something to drink. In doing this, you will heap burning coals of shame on their heads" (Romans 12:20).

We are to leave matters up to God
We are to place them in God's hands
Bring them before His throne of grace
He is our avenger
We are to leave all revenge to Him
Isn't this what Jesus taught?

In and off ourselves, this is impossible

This is why a relationship with God is so vital

When we are related to God through His Son, Jesus Christ, God gives us His Spirit to equip us, empower us, enable us to go through the battle—and the battles

When we act

React

What is produced in us are wounds

The real wounds!

The wounds that are tantamount to sin

That are sin

Anger

Hatred

Bitterness

Resentment

A desire for revenge

A spirit of un-forgiveness

Other wounds that are just as prevalent and costly to our lives are

Greed or covetousness

Pride

Any type of pride

These are the real wounds

These are the sins

The start-ups in our lives

The embryonic sins that start us down the path that can become even more hazardous and perilous

More dangerous to our spiritual health

And more deadly and consequential to both our physical and spiritual lives

This is where and when we enter the dark and dangerous territory of the scars

There is so much we can explore and discuss on this subject!

My prayer is that this is coming home to us—to you, the reader—

A lack of love and forgiveness

These two

"Twins," really

Are what is so egregiously wrong with our world today!

Wounds!

Again

What happens to us

What happens to us at the hands of others

These things are not the real wounds

They may feel like wounds

We may treat them as such

To us, they are

We say perception is reality

However, as tough as they are

As painful as they can be

Hard to get over

They are

Again

Life!

They stem from life, and what life has become

From being in life

Being in the battle

Against enemies that are, as Paul says, in the unseen world

Not all our battles

But some come to bring glory to God

But many are a part of this battle we are locked into

We will discuss Job later and why God got a little bit peeved

Miffed

At Job

To be clear

The real wounds come from how we respond to the battle—and the battles

These wounds

The ones that defile us

They come from within us!

When we respond

Or respond negatively

Or in kind

That's really when we suffer the wounds

They are self-inflicted wounds
That's the other thing
The wounds we suffer or experience in life are all self-inflicted
They are the sins that are conceived within us

> And remember, when you are being tempted, do not say, "God is tempting me." God is never tempted to do wrong, and he never tempts anyone else. Temptation comes from our own desires, which entice us and drag us away. These desires give birth to sinful actions. And when sin is allowed to grow, it gives birth to death (James 1:12-15).

So the wounds are the sins that are conceived inside of us
Everything else is life
The life we are in
The life that life has become
And we know that life
Early on in the life of our existence
Became what it is today—a battle

I know this is tough
Saying that what we experience—what we cast as wounds—is nothing more than life
Life happening to us
That what we go through is just life
But let's stop and think about it for a brief moment
Life

The battle
And the battles we face
What are they
Pain
Sickness
Diseases
Blindness
Lameness
Deafness
Dying
Death
Evil spirits (demons)
The devil
Temptations
Sin
And the like
All of these things are not a part of the Kingdom of God
Our ideal life with God
What life was like before humans sinned in the Garden
Jesus brought the Kingdom to earth with Him
He was the Kingdom
Jesus said, for instance, that the enemy
The devil
Had no part in Him
All of the aforementioned things are a part of life

And we say again—what life has become
What life is—now!

Jesus came
Among other things
To reveal the Kingdom of God
He was the Kingdom
None of these things had any part in Him
As a matter of fact
And with a command
He made all of them to just disappear
So much so that it made His disciples exclaim
"Who is this man?" they asked. "Even the winds and waves obey him!"
So is life in the Kingdom of God
The Kingdom of God transcends life
It's this other world
This other life, so to speak
This is what should make being a part of the Kingdom of God so attractive to us
It is God's way of life
It is ideal living
Completely the opposite
Antithetical!
To this miserable and dying world we live in

All of the things mentioned in our list above

Again, they are not the real wounds of this life

These are things that plague life

We can go back and read God's judgment—the judgment we humans brought upon ourselves

Genesis chapter 3

Here is more good news

Perhaps the greatest news of all!

God has a way of turning our battles

The hurt

The pain

The rejection

The injustices

And the abuses

All of it!

Into victories

Triumph

Success

Even our promotion!

What we perceive as wounds are actually tests

Opportunities

God uses

Well, he wants to use

The battle

What it has become

And the battles we face

To test us

Grow us

Mature us

Improve us

Grow our faith

Our character

(Oh, there is so much to tell about these things!)

Suffice it to say, right now—and as we will learn as we go along—God always meets us at the intersection of our battles and our wounds

CHAPTER 2

Life

So the "slings and arrows" that we suffer in life and at the hands of others, the wrongs

The abuses

The mistreatments

The injustices

These are all a part of the battle

A part of life

What's to be expected

What we can—and—should expect out of life

From life

What we should expect from being physically alive on planet Earth!

So the pains and heartaches and the strife and the abuses—these, my friends, are not the real wounds in and of this life

If we have not accepted this truth

It behooves us to

Then we will be better able to respond to life!

The real wounds stem from how we allow the things that happen to us in life to affect us

Bother us

Get to us

Get under our skin

Anger us

The real wounds are what the "injustices" and the "wrongs" suffered in battles—our perceptions—do to us

It's what the injustices and the wrongs suffered in battles do to us

What they create in us

And indeed, they can create "monsters" out of us!

It's what they create in us that are the real wounds

When we allow what happens to us in life

When we allow what others do to us to create in us the feelings and realities that are

Anger

Bitterness

Hatred

Jealousy

A desire for revenge

The spirit of unforgiveness

These are the real wounds of this life

These are the real wounds that can so easily turn into scars

Elongated challenges and issues for us

It is critical for us to understand that our wounds can and do turn into scars

Scars

Scars are the wounds that get stretched, extended, drawn out in our lives

That take root

Suddenly or over time

The scars

We will learn

Are the wounds that won't heal

The wounds that won't heal precisely because we do not allow them to heal

We may not have the love of God in us

Or we fail to properly exercise the love and forgiveness, the power, and the gift that God has blessed us with

we have to be led by the Spirit of God--not our own nature--our own sinful nature

The power

And the gift that God has blessed us with

This gift—stemming from His profound

Unfathomable

Wide and deep love
Is the power to choose

I believe with every fiber of my being that God is saying to us today
Our greatest challenges are the things we accept as minuscule
That we overlook
Love
Forgiveness
Basic goodness and decency
We are out there railing against what we perceive as the "big" sins
What about these sins
All sins!
The ones that can slip up on us so easily
Wrestle us down to the ground
Get the upper hand over us
Control us
The ones that can also lead to our demise
Just like any other sin
These are the real wounds that cost us dearly
Again, they can lead to our physical and spiritual demise
These are the real wounds that are devastatingly dangerous
These are the real wounds that can easily turn into far worse wounds

"Far worse wounds" being what the "wounds" suffered in battle turn into

This is what we mean when we say battles produce wounds—and wounds can and do turn into scars

Our wounds can easily turn into scars!

So easily that we may not even realize it

This is why prayer is so important

So important to the believer

The scars are
Wounds that are prolonged
Anger that is allowed to persist
Hate that rises, cooks, burns, and grows
Jealousy that grows and becomes twisted
A spirit of un-forgiveness that takes on a life of its own
That becomes a weight
A burden in our lives
The scars are what are dangerous
The scars are what are devastating to us
The scars are what rob us of life
Cause us to withdraw from life
Feel a sense of loneliness
Cause us to slip into depression
Make us sick
Physically
Emotionally

Psychologically

And most importantly, spiritually

The scars can cause us to lose sleep

They can rob us of our productivity

They can also rob us of our God-given purpose and potential

The scars!

This is how dangerous and deadly they are

Let me say rather quickly that I believe this is the reason why God led me to write this book

To point out the hidden dangers of these wounds

The scars

The negative feelings, emotions, and twisted desires that we allow to possess us

Take over and clutter our lives

Take up residency

Control us

Cause us to lose control

To spiral out of control

Take us out there on that "slippery slope of life" where we can easily lose control of our lives

Anger

Jealousy

Bitterness

Resentment

Hatred

Rage

Desire for revenge

Unwillingness to forgive

Pride

Covetousness, or greed

These are the real wounds we suffer in life!

Jesus

Touching on just one of these wounds

Anger

Jesus had this to say:

> You have heard that our ancestors were told, "You must not murder. If you commit murder, you are subject to judgment." But I say, if you are even angry with someone you are subject to judgment!
>
> If you call someone an idiot (a product of anger), you are in danger of being brought before the court. And if you curse someone (again, a product of anger), you are in danger of the fires of hell" (Matthew 5:21-22, parentheticals mine).

Why is Jesus talking about anger in this way?

Not because anger is intrinsically bad or even avoidable

But Jesus wants us to see what something as small and natural to us can turn into!

These wounds that can so easily turn into scars may spring up as a response to what we may perceive as a wound

What we may perceive as an injury

An injustice

But I believe God wants to remind us of the "little things"
Yes
The seemingly "innocent"
"harmless" things
That may not seem to have an effect on us but actually do
(All sin is sin in the eyes of God!
And we cannot hide our sins from God!)

I believe that it is the scars
The wounds
The negative build-ups that we allow to occur in our lives that are responsible for more death and destruction than all of the wars, conflicts, acts of terrorism, diseases, pestilences, droughts and famines, plagues, viruses, and pandemics combined

Again, life is a battle
As a battle, it produces other battles
Battles produce wounds
Wounds can and do turn into scars
However, our battles don't have to turn into scars
Good news alert!
Yes, it is possible to go through the battles without the scars!
Jesus would tell His disciples
Every time they would go through a storm
A difficulty

A challenging time or situation
In other words, a battle
He would tell them to have no fear
Take heart
Have courage
For he showed them—and us
Modeled for us
How to overcome
How to go through the battles
We must believe
Believe in God!
This is true faith!
Have faith in God
Rely on God

We are to rely on God, not ourselves!
Isn't it good to know that the battle—and the battles we go through in life—are winnable?
That we can successfully go through them
And thus overcome them
Triumph over the battles
Now can you picture the three Hebrew boys
Shadrach, Meshach, and Abednego
Walking around in the fire
With a fourth figure!
The one that looked like and was the Son of God!

Come on
If you believe it
And receive it
Give God some praise!

The good news is not that we can avoid the battles
The good news is that we can *go through the battles successfully*
Not affected by the scars
I want you to just ponder
Reflect on what it means
When the scripture says:

> So Shadrach, Meshach, and Abednego stepped out of the fire. Then the high officers, officials, governors, and advisers crowded around them and saw that the fire had not touched them. Not a hair on their heads was singed, and their clothing was not scorched. They didn't even smell of smoke! (Daniel 3:26-27).

Again, Jesus said
Battles will come
Storms will come
But we can go through the storms successfully
We can triumph over the storms of this life—even as we go through them
As long as God is in the boat with us
In our lives in the form of His Holy Spirit!

I believe the reason God gave me this book to write is so that the truth would come out

The truth about life

The battle

And the battles

And how to go through them

The Bible says

John 8:32

And you will know the truth, and the truth will set you free."

We Are Not Spared the Battles

We should shout about this, too!

Here is something we don't hear preached often from pulpits

Even though it is at the center of Jesus' teachings

The Word of God

We don't get to go around the storms or the battles

We all will have to go through them

However, some of us will go through the battles

And the storms

More successfully than others

This is why a relationship with God is so critical

So crucial

And so vital

This is why it is absolutely necessary to have a deep and abiding relationship with God

A covenant relationship with God

To have been redeemed

Purchased by God

Having been redeemed, chosen by God

And

Following Him faithfully is what allows us to safely and successfully go through the battles

Survive the storms

Withstand the fire

This is important!

The most kind and loving promises of God are not meant for everyone

Just the people of God

Jesus

The Word of God

Did not come to the world

If you and I want to benefit from the most enveloping and precious love of God, then we need to get out of the world and attach ourselves to the Source of all life

In the book of Exodus chapter 15
It says:

> The LORD is a warrior; Yahweh is his name!

Your right hand, O LORD, is glorious in power. Your right hand, O LORD, smashes the enemy. In the greatness of your majesty, you overthrow those who rise against you. You unleash your blazing fury. It consumes them like straw.

Who is like you among the gods, O LORD—glorious in holiness, awesome in splendor, performing great wonders?

With your unfailing love you lead the people you have redeemed (Exodus 15:3, 6-7, 11, 13).

CHAPTER 3

The Scars

I became aware of the scars early on in my life

How important they are

How dangerous they can become

And what a powerful role they play in our lives

It took just one incident—an almost innocent and innocuous event

Yet it was an event that would change my life forever

Reveal something illuminating about me, and, in the process, teach me an all-important lesson about life

I was a wounded and reckless soul

I had returned home one summer break from college

It was a time of real frustration for me

I had just recently broken up with my girlfriend of four and a half years—my college sweetheart—someone whom I had envisioned spending the rest of my life together with, someone I was madly in love with

However, God had other plans for me

The whole experience would teach me a very important principle about love and dating, marriage, and life

And that is—

that the better plan for our lives is always to go with, not the one that we love the most, but the one God has chosen and who loves us the most

This is order

God's order for our lives

This is how and when we discover the true love of God!

This principle is exemplified in the earthly life of Jesus and His two beloved disciples, Peter and John

You can say that I was wounded

I felt hurt

Crushed

Deceived

Rejected

Dumped

Betrayed

You name it

This "wounded state" would plunge me into a feeling of loneliness

Sadness

Depression

Helplessness

And despair

Little did I know—or realize—that I was just in the grips of life

That what was happening to me was life

It was the most serious rupture I had ever experienced in my young life

All I knew was that something was wrong

Something was amiss in my life

I can still vividly remember the incident

The depressing time

Again, the feeling of being alone, crushed, devastated, hurt, and angry

The unmistakable tinge yet brooding feeling of loneliness that hung over my life like a pallor

A feeling of being all alone in a vast, empty space

In short, as I stated, I was a wounded soul

At this stage of my life, I had not yet worked out the reality of life as a battle

How it produces, manufactures, spawns, and creates other battles

How, in the normal course of life, we become wounded

I was a young man, somewhat wild and carefree

As far as I was concerned, life was just not meant to be all that complicated

The Incident

I was driving home late one night after having tried to assuage my feelings of depression with a few beers and some old friends at a bar

I was driving rather vacuously

And as I rounded one of the many roundabouts in the city, not paying much attention to my own slightly erratic driving, I thought I felt this other car in the next lane—just slide over and bump my car

It felt more like a jolt

Keep in mind that confusion was already reigning in my world

My emotions were already sensitive, raw, and in a swirl

Depression, anger, and the deep feelings of loneliness had already taken up residence in my troubled mind

Anger

Anger is something that can spring up in an instant

It's an emotional reaction that forms as a result of what goes on in our hearts or our minds, the seat of our emotions and desires

Our all-too-human emotions and desires are not good

It is what the Bible refers to as the flesh

Nothing good is conceived there

Anger—And What It Can Lead To!

When that other car "bumped" me, in a way, it snapped me back to the moment

My quiet, suppressed anger woke up

Immediately, I flew into a rage

To make matters worse, the occupants in the other car—young, presumably tourists on vacation—seemed to be having a rollicking good time

Windows all rolled down

Waving articles of light clothing in the air

They were having the time of their lives—laughing, singing, and punctuating the air with their hands

A real air of carefree, aery gaiety

Here I was, feeling like my life had become unhinged, torn loose from its tethers and moorings, and these people flaunting their frivolity all up in my face

Carefree and recklessly careless

Something that I have learned is that when we are sliding toward depression, our emotions are splayed, frayed, and very much on edge

Sensitive to almost any provocation

Like a cavity is to cold or hot

Incensed, I swung my car in behind them and stabbed my foot on the accelerator

And the chase was on!

I have since discovered that it is truly amazing how easily and quickly a wound, real or imagined, can turn into a scar—a heightened, intensified, intense, hardened, crystalized wound that just sets in, that grips you

That won't leave

The Scar

The scar is a wound

It is a wound that can progress quickly or slowly

It is a wound that we allow to set in

It is a wound that sits and festers

It is a wound that won't heal

It is a wound that we allow to not heal

Yes, the scars are wounds

Wounds that we suffer

That are produced inside of us

They oftentimes stem from what we perceive to be a wound

So they can be real or imagined

Wounds sting

They hurt

And cause us pain

Emotional pain

Emotional pain that can lead to a train wreck

Wounds that we feel are wrong bear the "sting" and all the "marks of injustice"
They cry out for our own form of justice
Some form of revenge

An Explosive Moment

I was a wounded soul
Now doubly and freshly wounded
Or so I thought
I chased that car that I *thought* had rammed my car all the way to the hotel where the occupants were staying
I came to a screeching halt, jumped out of the car, and, like a ranting, raving lunatic, I started yelling and flailing my arms wildly at the driver and passengers.
Bewildered and confused at first, they just stood there and glared
Suddenly, their joyful, celebratory mood had become deflated, all of the air sucked out of it
All because of me
I could see several of them inching away, stepping back, not knowing what to make of this sudden turn of events
Not sure where it was headed
I was furious
I cannot remember ever being so angry in all my life
And yes—I was a ranting, raving lunatic
I was angry—yes

But more so, I was troubled

Hurt

Wounded

Injured

At one point, I remember slamming on the hood of my own car and demanding that somebody come and take a look at the damage they had done

I didn't know if that hotel had security cameras or not

But if they did—and played it back later—I must have looked like an abject fool

Except for a couple of the men, the passengers had all managed to make their escape

They had quietly slipped into the confines of the hotel lobby

A few other guests stood at a safe distance

Their jaws hanging wide open

Eyes bulging

They, too, could not believe what they were witnessing

It was a moment of suspension

I, too, was suspended

Not completely in control of my emotions

Feeling them slip away the angrier I became

One of the gentlemen, the driver of the car, apparently, was brave enough to come around the vehicle to try and reason with me

To "calmly and rationally discuss the situation"

"What seems to be the problem, sir?" he asked

"Oh no! Don't you try to get all smug with me!" I heard my voice ringing inside my head

I was hot

Fuming

"What seems to be the problem?" I retorted

My voice coming back to me

And taking umbrage to what—to me—sounded like fake politeness and sincerity

Pugnacious tourists, I thought

I became even more enraged

I was fuming!

"You are asking me 'what seems to be the problem'?"

I repeated the question several times

"Didn't you see you guys just rammed my car back there coming around that roundabout?"

"I'm sorry, sir, but I was the one driving, and I didn't realize we had hit your car. However, if we did, we would be more than happy to pay for the damages"

I wanted him to know that he had hurt me—well, hurt my car, anyway

"You hit my car!" I fumed

I was hot and felt like I was about to explode

Reflections on Anger

Anger can be a dangerous thing, especially when you feel— you are convinced—that you have been wronged

Anger can quickly explode

Turn into something else

More dangerous

More destructive

Even deadly

When this happens, it is hard to control

Hard to gain control over

It is also at this volatile point that the wound can easily turn into a scar

Again, a scar is a wound

It is a wound that grows and festers

That escalates

A scar can be a masked wound that we carry

That we allow to grow in our lives

That we allow to grow and fester

A scar is a wound that we allow to negatively impact our lives

Carry around with us

Like a weight, a baggage, or a burden

Finally, a scar is a wound that we allow to just sit, grow, and fester

And—this is very important—we do not allow to heal

We all have moments when we get angry

Anger is not necessarily a bad thing

And there are different types of anger

The danger comes when we allow our anger to escalate
To get the better of us
Anger is a product of our emotions
Our all-too-very-human emotions

Since this incident, I have come to lean on this verse from scripture:

> Human anger does not produce the righteousness
> God desires (James 1:20).

The Revelation

So I escorted the gentleman over to the front and around to the side of my car
"Look! Right there!" I shouted
We both leaned in
I wanted him to see what—I was absolutely certain—must have been a significant, caved-in, scraped-up, or dented front fender
I wanted him to see the damage
The damage done to me
What I was feeling
Which was the hurt and pain they had caused me
I wanted him to see the stark evidence

However, much to my extreme surprise, dismay, and embarrassment, not a single mark or scrape was visible anywhere on the car

I looked

I looked again

Leaned in even closer

Blinked

I wiped away the little bit of caked-on dirt and dust from the side of the car

And I stared at the clean, blank spot, unable to believe my eyes

Anger is real

You can feel that someone has done you wrong

Embarrassment is also real and palpable

I was frozen

Stupefied

This could not be happening

Needless to say, I felt like an utter fool

For the first time that evening, I was at a total loss for words

Life Is a Battle

It produces, manufactures, spawns, and creates other battles

Battles Produce Wounds

Our wounds can be real or imagined

Let's just say

For argument sake

Real or imagined, they are all wounds

That is because, real or imagined, they have their effect on us

They hurt

They sting

They ache

Wounds can and do turn into scars

Sudden escalations, heightening and deepening of the initial "wound"

Our perceived wounds too often turn into real wounds that won't heal

Wounds that we allow to escalate

To grow and to fester

Our wounds, when they elongate in our lives and turn into scars, are ever more dangerous

They are dangerous precisely because they can cause us to see stars, so to speak

Lose control

Spiral out of control

Lead us out onto a "slippery slope"

A slippery slope in our minds

That slippery slope of life

Out on this slippery slope or ledge, we lose control

We lose control of our thinking and our ability to think, reason

We lose control of our "faculties"

Once at this point emotionally, our lives can spin even more out of control

Causing us to lose all control

The loss of complete control—it never fails—leads to a less-than-desirable and ignoble end

Right there and then, it all became crystal clear to me

It hit me

The "wound"—the hurt that I was feeling inside, the sad experience of the breakup with my girlfriend—that was not the real wound

The real wound was what the feeling

The feeling of being wounded

Had produced in me

The "wound" had turned into a wound that was real

A more dangerous, potentially deadly wound

My life was in danger

The enemy had intervened

And was coaxing

And encouraging me

But God had mercy on me that night!

My life was spiraling out of control

I was feeling lonely, hurt, depressed, and angry

Not from this incident, but the prior one

The big one

This incident with the car was simply a trigger

What We Perceive as Wounds— and the Trigger Effect

The things that triggered my wound

Woken it up

Poured salt on the wound

Tore the scab off

Exposed the "wound" that had not healed

The hurt

The pain

The rejection

The feeling of loneliness and depression

I came to realize that deep down, I was still aching, hurting, and depressed

That I was carrying this pent-up anger and frustration around with me, looking for some hapless souls or situation to just dump it on

And just like that

My perceived wound had turned into a real wound

A scar

The real wound was my anger

Which, in an instant, had turned into rage

A desire for revenge

I came to realize that our wounds, in the blink of an eye, can quickly turn into a dangerous and deadly scar

Scars can turn us into emotional wrecks

Out-of-control bulldozers

I was an out-of-control bulldozer about to spin completely out of control

I think we all know the extent of damage an out-of-control bulldozer can do!

I came to realize that I could have killed someone that night

Or someone could have killed me

Again

That moment was the first time I came to see the nature of the wound

The real wound

That emotional phenomenon

Which is anger

Which is a potentially dangerous and deadly wound

And how it can so easily turn into a scar

The scar is a wound that won't heal

A wound that we choose to carry

Hold on to

The scar is a wound that just won't heal because we refuse to allow it *to* heal

I came to realize that life is a battle

It produces battles

We will all go through these battles

And

It's our battles that produce the wounds

Both what we perceive as wounds

And the actual wounds

We are not responsible for the battles we will go through in life

It's the nature of the battle

It's life

Battles produce wounds

The perceived ones

And the real ones

We are not always responsible for the wounds we suffer in life

However, our wounds do not have to turn into scars

This is the message

The good news

The real message of this book!

That incident was also the first time I came to realize that we live our lives at the intersection of our battles and our wounds

A busy intersection indeed!

What happens at this intersection of our lives can and will shape our lives forever and all eternity

It will determine our destiny

The wounds are dangerous and deadly because of their potential to turn into far worse wounds

The metamorphosis of the wound into a scar

The Nurtured Wounds Are a Continuation of Sin

The wounds are special, not in a good way

They are sin

They are special precisely because they, like no other sins, are in our care

Under our control

God has given us a measure of responsibility for our wounds

God does not give us full control over our lives, of course

He reserves that for Himself

However, God wants us to experience the joy of sovereignty that He has

This is His desire

This has always been His plan and His desire for our lives

Even if it means—and leads to—vulnerability

His vulnerability

Vulnerability is a sign and the mark of love

Love makes us vulnerable

God is love

It all comes back to love

And Love!

The key to life is how we respond to the wounds we suffer in life

We will discuss this topic in connection with Cain later on in the book

The wounds are the areas that God has given us some control over

God has given us this responsibility

This freedom

This opportunity to discover Him

God wants us to live our lives in peace, first of all

God wants us to live our lives in freedom

But freedom with—at all times—responsibility

(Let this be a message—and a warning—to our societies!)

This involves even the freedom to choose or deny God

Go with Him or against Him

So the wounds are our areas of opportunity and testing

God has given us some control over our wounds

How we respond to them

Again

I repeat

The real wounds are not the

Hurt

Wrongs

Injuries

Injustices

Pain

Suffering

Insults

Bad Treatment

Mistreatment

Abuses

That we experience in life

No, the real wounds are what those perceived wounds create or produce in us

Wounds such as

Anger

Bitterness

Resentment

Hatred

Rage

Jealousy

A desire for revenge

A spirit of unforgiveness

Pride or lack of humility

Covetousness or greed

Our "wounds"

The ones that we see and focus on are the realities, the sad realities, and conditions produced by life

They can be—to us—just as real as the real wounds!

That is, when we go through "stuff"

When others hurt us or wrong us

It really doesn't matter whether the wound is real or imagined

They all sting
They all hurt
Ache
And pain us

Our response to the hurts, aches, and pains is what engenders the real wound
The real wounds can cause us to become disoriented
Discombobulated
And
As we have been saying now
These wounds
Real and imagined
Can and do lead to scars!

The Scars Are the Wounds That Have Progressed

For example, the wound of anger can turn into rage
Unrelenting anger and rage
Which, when it locks in, becomes the scar
Today, we have invented the word "road rage"

The painful nature—and the chaotic nature of our wounds—can also bring pain and suffering, not just to our lives but also to the lives of others
Again
It cannot be overstated

Or stated enough

It is at the point of our battles and our wounds where we live our lives

Sometimes

Very dangerously

This is also the point at which we make critical decisions that can alter and change our lives forever

This is where we can succumb to the evil thoughts and forces that are seeking to lead us astray, derail us

Destroy us

This is where we have to be careful so that we don't lose control

So that our lives don't spiral out of control

This is where we need to be careful with the "voices" that we hear inside our heads, egging us on

This is where we need an anchor, an anchor that grips, an anchor that holds

This is where we need a moral compass

True and reliable

A moral compass that will influence our thoughts, actions, and behaviors

This is where we need Truth

Truth that dictates right from wrong

The arbitration of right and wrong in our lives

A regulator

As God said to Cain

> Why are you so angry? . . . Why do you look so dejected? You will be accepted if you do what is right. But if you refuse to do what is right, then watch out! Sin is crouching at the door, eager to control you (Genesis 4:6-7).

Satan wants to get in on our wounded journey

What could be our precipitous slide

It's his party

He relishes the moment

When we are down

Depressed

Feeling lonely and all distraught

Changed forever

As humbly as I could that night, I apologized to the gentleman

Begged his forgiveness

Asked him to please extend my apologies to his party

Told him how sorry I was for ruining their evening

Then I got back in my car and drove—rather, skulked—away

Broken

Dejected

And utterly humiliated

I just felt like crying

However, without realizing it then, I had just learned the most wonderful and valuable lesson of my life

CHAPTER 4

Perceived and Real Wounds

We are saying it—adumbrating it
I am a teacher
I cannot help myself
I know that redundancy has its value
So just bear with me
Yes
We have been saying
Stressing
That battles produce wounds
And this is true
But what do we mean by this?
What are the wounds produced in battles?
There are two types of wounds in this life

Wounds that we perceive as wounds

And the wounds that are real

The wounds that are perceived—we have already dealt with

They are not the actual wounds

They parade around in our minds as real wounds

But they are not the real wounds

The ones touching our spirit and our souls

Directing and redirecting the course of our spirit and our souls

Shaping our destiny

The real wounds are those that penetrate deep down to the spirit and soul level

Wounds that can truly affect our lives

Cause us pain

Grief

Conflict

The loss of peace

Inner peace

Joy, happiness

A lack of a purposeful life

Death

Truly imperil our lives

Even our God-given potential and purpose

These wounds that are deeply spiritual do not stem from what we perceive to be wounds

What happens to us
Or what others have done to us
Life
The wrongs
The hurts
The pains
Injustices
Bad treatment
Mistreatment
Abuse
All forms of abuses
What are, in effect, the fallout of the battle and the battles we face
Again
These perceived wounds stem from
The hurts
The pains
The wrongs
The injustices
The mistreatments
Bad treatments
Being lied on
And cheated on
The many forms of abuses

These are not the real wounds but can be the source or the root of our wounds

They are what can create in us the real wounds!

Wounds that carry with them repercussions and consequences

Serious repercussions and consequences!

The real wounds are what happens inside of us

Bubbles up inside of us

Come to life in us

After our perceived wounds

Emotions and desires such as

Anger

Hatred

Bitterness

Resentment

Rage

Jealousy

A desire for revenge

A spirit of unforgiveness

Pride or lack of humility

Covetousness or greed

They create in us the real wounds when we decide to act

React

React negatively

Or in kind to the perceived wounds

When we decide to react

Go tit for tat

Lash out

Take matters into our own hands

Ignore principles

The Word of God

Because that is what the Word of God is

Principles!

Principles for us to live by!

We can't always control what happens to us

But we can control how we respond to what happens to us

Our Wounds Are Spiritual

Battles are spiritual

The wounds that we allow to take root inside of us are spiritual

Deeply spiritual

They have spiritual ramifications and consequences

We should never let the blows or the injuries we suffer in battle be confused with the wounds produced by the battle or the battles

The real wounds are not what we experience in life

The real wounds are not what happens to us

Even though they leave us feeling hurt, injured, and wronged

These wounds that we perceive as wounds are merely part of the battle

What we must go through in life

They happen

They are to be expected

They are a reflection of what life has become

The real wounds occur when we react

When we respond to these attacks

When we respond in kind

Reacting brings out, for lack of a better term, the "ugliness" in us

The not-so-pleasant

What we should not allow to dwell in our lives

The emotions and desires that can grip us

Control us

And possess us, even

These are not-like-God characteristics

Characteristics that demonstrate love

Who God is

Who God wants us to be

Can you imagine what would have happened if God's love was reactionary?

We would all still be dead in our sins

Without any hope at all!

It is better to suffer the perceived wounds

It is better to accede right of way

Go the extra mile

Turn the proverbial other cheek

God is in control

He is our avenger

He will fight all of our battles for us

We just have to submit to Him

Surrender our lives to Him

Come into agreement with Him

Be obedient to His commands

Give our lives over to Him

In other words, love Him

Now we understand what Jesus meant when He said in Matthew 5:38-42:

> You have heard the law that says the punishment must match the injury: 'An eye for an eye, and a tooth for a tooth.' But I say, do not resist an evil person! If someone slaps you on the right cheek, offer the other cheek also. If you are sued in court and your shirt is taken from you, give your coat, too. If a soldier demands that you carry his gear for a mile, carry it two miles. Give to those who ask, and don't turn away from those who want to borrow.

The problem is that we sometimes react without fully and completely thinking the matter through

We let our emotions get in the way

Get the better part of us

We fail to reflect

We fail to reflect upon God and His Word

We are left only to imagine

What if David

As he stood on that balcony

Peering out at Bathsheba, who was taking a bath

Had reflected

What if Saul

Rather than allowing his anger and jealousy toward David to come into his heart, had reflected

We simply ignore God's universal and timeless truths

By the way, His timeless and universal truths

Principles

Are designed to keep us safe

Grow us

Prosper us

Form the beauty that is character in us

When Wounds Turn into Scars

So the wounds are what is produced inside of us as a result of our battles

For example, when we go through battles and we suffer or experience what we perceive as wounds, we tend to get angry

We tend to allow anger and hatred to come in, to seep in

Jealousy

Extreme anger

Bitterness

Resentment

A desire for revenge

A spirit of unforgiveness

These are the real wounds of this life

What we allow to come into our lives

Jesus illustrated this principle of the wound

What are the real wounds in life, beautifully

Listen to our Lord explain it

> Then Jesus called to the crowd to come and hear. "Listen," he said, "and try to understand. It's not what goes into your mouth that defiles you; you are defiled by the words that come out of your mouth" (Matthew 15:10-11).

Then again:

> "Don't you understand yet?" Jesus asked. "Anything you eat passes through the stomach and then goes into the sewer. But the words you speak come from the heart—that's what defiles you. For from the heart come evil thoughts, murder, adultery, all sexual immorality, theft, lying, and slander. These are what defile you. Eating with unwashed hands will never defile you" (Matthew 15:16-20).

What Jesus was saying, in effect, was that food is something that happens to us

In life, we eat

What happens to us is not what really affects us

What affects us are those things that we have been talking about

As our Lord said

It is from the heart that comes evil thoughts

Murder

Adultery

All sexual immorality

Theft

Lying

And slander

These are the things that defile us

The wounds

The sins that, once they become scars, can cause us real harm

Again

The wounds are what are formed within us

That we allow to take over our lives

Control us

That become manifest into thoughts, actions, and behaviors

And cause us to sin

They cause us to sin precisely because these are the wounds

The spiritual wounds

That we allow to grow

Develop

Fester

Take root

These are the wounds that start out as wounds but develop and turn into even worse wounds

We call these worse wounds that can develop and take root scars

The wounds—and the scars—are our negative and damaging reactions to our battles

Remember, we have very little control over what happens to us

What happens to us in battle

What we do have control over is how we respond to the battle

What happens to us

How we respond is what leads to—or not—the wound or wounds

God has already given us His Word

His instructions

What the Bible calls "laws, statutes, and decrees"

Today, we say principles

Guidelines on how we are to respond to life

This

His Word

Is where we see most clearly how God wants us to respond to life

The battle

The first humans sinned

This set up a chain reaction

The Bible says in Romans 5:

> When Adam sinned, sin entered the world. Adam's sin brought death, so death spread to everyone, for everyone sinned (12).
>
> Yes, Adam's one sin brings condemnation for everyone . . . Because one person disobeyed God, many became sinners (18–19).

Sin Is Rebellion

We who are sinners—and we all are, except for and through God's grace—are

In our natural state

At war with God

The Bible says:

> "For everyone has sinned; we all fall short of God's glorious standard" (Romans 3:23).

But the Bible also says:

> "But God showed his great love for us by sending Christ to die for us while we were still sinners" (Romans 5:8).

So even though we were living our lives contrary to God

Locked in battle with Him

Still at war with Him

God still showed His great love for us

We have to keep in mind that God is love

Love does not react

Love just does what He does

Loves!

> "For this is how God loved the world: He gave his one and only Son, so that everyone who believes in him will not perish but have eternal life" (John 3:16)

Now, we can spurn God's love

Reject His love

Even abandon Him

But that does not mean God will abandon us

God does not abandon what He loves

The Bible says that God remains faithful even if we all are found to be

Turn out to be

Unfaithful:

> "If we are unfaithful, He remains faithful" (2 Timothy 2:13).

For He cannot deny who He is

The verse just above this one states

> "This is a trustworthy saying: If we die with him, we will also live with him. If we endure hardship, we will reign with him" (2 Timothy 2:11-12).

Death and dying are a part of life

They are a part of the battle

When we "endure" hardship, it means that we don't react to it

We don't allow the "wounds" to turn into scars

When we go through the battles without the scars, then—and only then—will we achieve real and lasting success

We will reign with Him!

Again, we can and do abandon God

Which, in turn, brings judgment on ourselves

However, that is not the same as God abandoning us

As a matter of fact, God does not cause judgment

Sin produces judgment

The Bible says:

> "For the wages of sin is death, but the free gift of God is eternal life through Christ Jesus our Lord" (Romans 6:23).

Sin leads to judgment and death

God does not cause death and judgment

As a matter of fact, God only brings us good things

Gifts

> "Whatever is good and perfect is a gift coming down to us from God our Father, who created all the lights in the heavens" (James 1:17).

He never changes or casts a shifting shadow

> "He chose to give birth to us by giving us his true word. And we, out of all creation, became his prized possession" (James 1:18).

Left unchecked, wounds tend to turn into scars

Scars that are dangerous

Deadly

They stem from our battles

They are deeply spiritual

Other potentially self-destructive wounds include

Pride or lack of humility

Self-pride

Greed or covetousness

These are just some of the wounds—the effects of the battles and our perceived wounds—we experience or suffer in life

So first, we are "wounded" in battle

Then our "wound" or "wounds" from the battle produce in us a real and potentially deadly wound

These are the wounds that truly matter to God

The reaction to our battles and what we perceive as the wrongs or the injury or the injustice done to us

Again, the real wounds are not the hurts and pains we suffer in battle but what the hurts, the pains, the abuse, the injustices, and the wrongs produce in us

Cain's Perceived Wound

Cain thought he was wounded

He felt that he was wronged

Cain felt that God had done him an injustice

God was saying, on the other hand,

(and I paraphrase)

Suck it up, Cain!

This is life

You reap what you sow

In other words, God did not "wound" Cain or do him an injustice

His brother, Abel, did not do anything wrong to Cain

Cain "felt" he had been wronged!

That he had been wounded

This self-perception on the part of Cain is what led to his downfall

Which was created by his anger

His hatred

And his jealousy toward his brother, Abel

Our wounds

Or our internal response to what happens to us in battles is the potential onset of our scars

What is of real importance to God is how we respond to life and the situations that happen in life

This is what really matters to God

Not what happens to us in life

But how we respond to what happens to us

The same is true of Saul and David

(We will discuss these renowned biblical figures later)

Their battles

And what happened to them

Their "perceived" and "real" wounds

Their sins

Their wounds that turned into scars

Their spiritual wounds

CHAPTER 5

Wounds Have Spiritual Repercussions

Again, the wounds that we experience or suffer in life are not those things that happen to us

What happens to us is part of the battle

Life

The wounds

Our wounds

Come from how we respond to our battles

What happens to us internally

The feelings and emotions that well up inside of us

That burst of emotion

Or that slow burn of an emotion

That irrational, almost inexplicable desire

Negative, as far as God is concerned

(We can think back to David and Bathsheba here)

That irrational and almost inexplicable desire that is displeasing to God

These are the real wounds

They are the wounds that if we don't find healing for—and quick—can lead to our spiritual demise

Our spiritual death

The spiritual is more important than the physical

The spiritual

What takes place on the spirit level

Is what is real

It is the wounds that cause us to lose control

These are the wounds

That can cause us to self-destruct

Both physically and spiritually

And in the wake of our own tragic physical and spiritual demise, lead to a lot of other deaths and destruction

So the real wounds are the sins produced in us as a result of our battles

Things that we are to try and avoid at all cost if we are to live a successful, triumphant, victorious life

If we are to be promoted

Our promotion can come in this life and or the next

The wounds we experience or suffer are dangerous and potentially deadly emotions and desires, such as

Anger

Hatred

Resentment

Bitterness

Jealousy

A desire for revenge

A spirit of unforgiveness

Pride

Envy

Greed or covetousness

These, then, are the real wounds that we experience or suffer in life

That we internalize

They are wounds that can potentially turn into scars

Scars are more permanent, dangerous, and deadly wounds that may develop

They tend to manifest themselves in terrible, wrongful actions and behaviors

They can develop slowly

Or they can spring up in an instant

God does not want us living lives that are reactive

Paying back evil for evil

Taking revenge

The Bible says God is our avenger

> "Dear friends, never take revenge. Leave that to the righteous anger of God. For the Scriptures say, 'I will take revenge. I will pay them back,' says the LORD" (Romans 12:19).

It goes on to say:

> Instead, 'If your enemies are hungry, feed them. If they are thirsty, give them something to drink. In doing this, you will heap burning coals of shame on their heads.' Don't let evil conquer you, but conquer evil by doing good" (Romans 12:20-21).

By the way, this is exactly what Jesus taught

Nurturing Wounds Feeds Our Flesh

We have to be careful with our emotions and our desires

Hardly anything good comes from them

They can lead us down the wrong path to a dead-end

To disaster

Why?

Precisely because they belong to our sinful nature

The opposite of a perfect, God-like nature that we lost when life was turned into a battle

This sinful nature is what the Bible calls "the flesh"

Everything produced or conceived in our sinful flesh, the heart/mind, being a part of who we are

Our so-called flesh

Tends toward doing bad

Doing evil

The apostle Paul writes in Romans 7:

> "I know that nothing good lives in me, that is, in my sinful nature. I want to do what is right, but I can't. I want to do what is good, but I don't. I don't want to do what is wrong, but I do it anyway. But if I do what I don't want to do, I am not really the one doing wrong; it is sin living in me that does it. I have discovered this principle of life—that when I want to do what is right, I inevitably do what is wrong" (18-21).

But the apostle Paul does not stop there

He goes on to say:

> "Oh, what a miserable person I am! Who will free me from this life that is dominated by sin and death? Thank God! The answer is in Jesus Christ our Lord" (24-25).

This is also why the Bible says to lean not unto thine own understanding

It is in our hearts and in our minds that the wounds are produced

Conceived

We feel, or we believe, that we have been wronged

Someone has done us an injustice

The enemy comes alongside us to goad us on

Help to convince us even further that we have been wronged

That we are right to pursue justice

To seek and exact revenge

The Ultimate Battle Is a Spiritual One

We have said

Established

That there is a battle being fought at the center of life

This battle is really between the enemy

The devil

Satan

Who used to be known as Lucifer before he was kicked out of Heaven for rebellion

And God

So the battle is really between the enemy of life and God

In a sense

We are in the middle of the battle

Caught in the crosshairs

But we cannot—and should never forget—the battle that life got turned into was because of us humans

Not God!

Also

It is us who are in the grips of the enemy

Rocked and swayed by his overtures

His temptations

It is us that He seeks to enter

Possess

And destroy

What intensifies the battle is precisely because we are God's cherished creation

God loves and cares for us

The devil understands this too

God wants to see us successfully pass the test, so to speak

God through the battles and the battles

God wants to see us exert faith

Be obedient to Him and His Word

This is what pleases God

Faith in God and His Word can change the trajectory of our lives

Even our lives' destinies

Abraham is a perfect example

Our success

Our triumph over life—and what it has become

Fear

Doubt—the absence of faith

Our triumph over life

Is what pleases God

Yes, God wants to see us go through the battles without incurring the wounds/the scars

Then we will be truly blessed

Then we will have achieved true success

Experience real triumph

Then—and only then—will we have paved the way for our true promotion in this life and beyond

Then—and only then—will we be able to live our best lives

The Bible says in Philippians 2:

> "You must have the same attitude that Christ Jesus had. Though he was God, he did not think of equality with God as something to cling to. Instead, he gave up his divine privileges; he took the humble position of a slave and was born as a human being. When he appeared in human form, he humbled himself in obedience to God and died a criminal's death on a cross. Therefore, God elevated him to the place of highest honor and gave him the name above all other names, that at the name of Jesus every knee should bow, in heaven and on earth and under the earth, and every tongue declare that Jesus Christ is Lord, to the glory of God the Father" (5-11).

Again

Jesus is our model

He showed us

Paved the way for us

Demonstrated

Once and for all

Yet, in the clearest of fashion

How we are to go through the battle—and the battles without being damaged

Imperiled

By the scars

We are to live our lives with humility

Making sacrifices for one another
Putting others first
Just as Jesus did
Again
God
In Jesus
Demonstrated love
Compassion
Forgiveness
Overlooking our faults
God showed us
Clearly and demonstrably
What our stance
But not just what our stance should be
But how we are to act toward each other
It is the act that is the hallmark of true love
The Bible also says in Isaiah 53:5, 7

> But he was pierced for our rebellion (wounds), crushed for our sins. He was beaten so we could be whole. He was whipped so we could be healed. He was oppressed and treated harshly, yet he never said a word. He was led like a lamb to the slaughter. And as a sheep is silent before the shearers, he did not open his mouth (parenthetical mine).

Finally, it says in Luke 23:34
As Jesus hung on the cross

After enduring the slings and arrows of this life
After having gone through the battle
After being falsely accused and arrested
Lied on
Spat on
Jeered and ridiculed
Beaten and tortured
Made fun of
Nailed, hand and feet, to a cross
Hoisted
Crucified
For no sins/wounds that He had committed
Yet
He would say
Plead with the Father
While He was still on the cross
Just before He would die
An innocent man
At the hands of His accusers:

> "Father, forgive them . . ."

So the question remains
Can we go through life (both the battle and the battles) free of the wounds and scars?
Free of

Anger

Rancor

Bitterness

Resentment

Hatred

Jealousy

Prejudice that leads to discrimination

Pride

Self-pride

Covetousness or greed

A spirit of unforgiveness?

Yes, we can!

Jesus did!

Joseph did!

David, except for his sin with Bathsheba, did

These are all models for us

They represent the good news

Yes, we can go through the battle and the battles without the scars

But how?

How to Go through Battles without the Scars

How are we able to go through the battles without the scars?

First, it is only through the grace of God

Jesus Christ Himself is that grace of God

Secondly

In the power, strength, and humility that comes from God

It is never about us

It is never in and of ourselves

By us or through us

As a matter of fact, in and of ourselves

This life

This kind of living

This result

Is impossible

Only God heals

Only God can give us the strength and the power to go through the battles without the scars!

We cannot stress enough the power and absolute necessity of a deep and abiding relationship with God

Jesus says in John 15:5:

> "I am the vine; you are the branches. Those who remain in me, and I in them, will produce much fruit. For apart from me you can do nothing."

God wants us to live lives that are pure

Full of integrity

Free from perpetual wrongdoing

Integrity matters to God!

A life that is committed and obedient to God's every Word is important to Him

God is love

Love is pure

At peace

Free from any form of perversion, impurity, or contaminant

A Note About the Devil

The devil's aim, or goal, is to thwart the will of God

So when the wound is produced or conceived, the devil is right there

He is out to destroy the work in progress of God

Remember, the ultimate aim and goal of the enemy is to facilitate and preside over the destruction of what really matters to God—

The human soul

The enemy, or the devil, sees our wounds as important precisely because our wounds, when they turn into scars, can and will lead to the death and destruction of our souls

Again, when we allow these wounds to sit

Fester

And grow

They tragically turn into even deeper, dangerous, and more deadly wounds

They turn into scars

These are the wounds, along with the battles, that we see throughout the Bible

These are the wounds Jesus taught

Preached

And warned us about

Jesus' Disciples Followed in His Footsteps

They, too, taught, preached, and warned about the wounds—the scars

They did so because they understood the power

The consequential power of these wounds affecting our lives

They knew that the battle and the battles produced wounds

And they knew that the wounds could turn into deeper and far worse wounds

More permanent wounds

(With the enemy's help)

Dangerous and deadly wounds

Destructive wounds

It is these prolonged wounds

Wounds that we allow to develop, grow, and fester in our lives

That become scars

CHAPTER 6

Ministering to the Wounded

We have to discuss our ministry to those who have been wounded in battles

Or who feel they have

This

Knowing how to minister to those going through difficult times is critical

It must be a time of sensitivity

And delicacy

How do we minister to the one who feels like they have been wounded by life?

That someone else has done them a terrible injustice

That God has unjustly dealt them a grave injustice

How do you talk to the Naomis of this life

The Jobs

Naomi felt that life had dealt her a cruel hand
And it had
She lost her husband
Shortly after that, she lost both her sons
Everything she had, valued, and cherished in life
Naomi looked at it this way

> "Don't call me Naomi," she responded. "Instead, call me Mara, for the Almighty has made life very bitter for me. I went away full, but the LORD has brought me home empty. Why call me Naomi when the LORD has caused me to suffer and the Almighty has sent such tragedy upon me?" (Ruth 1:20-21).

Of course, Naomi was looking at things from the perspective that what had happened to her must have been of God because he allowed it

Naomi

A devout believer

Is not bitter

She is really saying that life has dealt her a cruel hand

She is accepting of her fate

She actually has a profound understanding of how life is a battle

Job

On the other hand

Is one of those interesting and curious stories

And characters

In the Bible

What can best be said about Job is that life happened to Job in a most terrible fashion

Again

Keep in mind that the devil

Trials

Tribulations

Temptations

These are all a part of life

The battle

Yes

We can say that life happened to Job in a sudden, cascading and most horrific fashion

We can feel nothing but compassion for Job

Life can be hard

Harsh

Unrelenting at times

Sometimes delivering a series of blows one after the other

Job's story begins with Satan, the tempter or the accuser, appearing before God to request permission to try Job

> One day the members of the heavenly court came to present themselves before the LORD, and the Accuser, Satan, came with them. "Where have you come from?" the LORD asked Satan. Satan answered the LORD, "I have been patrolling the earth, watching everything that's going on" (Job 1:6-7).

Then, a spate of calamities hit
One after another, Job's family was decimated[1]
Job is a stalwart
A champion of faith in the Bible
Job never wavered in his faith in God
The key to going through the battles without the scars

Job
Unlike Naomi
Failed to understand the full nature of life
Life as a battle
He has a vague idea

> Is not all human life a struggle? Our lives are like that of a hired hand, like a worker who longs for the shade, like a servant waiting to be paid (Job 7:1).

Job saw his life almost as a duel between him and God
Not as something that can happen to any of us
Job railed against God
Insinuated
Implied that it was God who was being unfair
We say all the time life is unfair, but is it really?
Life is life
With all of its challenges, difficulties, pain, and hardships
Le us not forget how life became what it is today--a battle

---
[1] Job 1:13-19

Life was turned into a battle because of sin!
Who sinned?
God did not turn life into a battle
Nor did the devil
Human sin did!
Our sin!
Is life really unfair?
So God had to straighten Job out
Explain a thing or two about life
That He, God, is sovereign
Everything He does is in love
God said to Job
In essence
Job
You just need to be quiet
Accept life
It happens to all of us
Just go through it without complaining so that in the next phase of your life on earth, I can bless you!
God was saying
Job
The key to life
And this is all you need to know, my child
Is to remain humble
Faithful

Obedient

And go through the battles without grumbling

Complaining

Like something about you is special

Unique

Who are you?

Mortal man!

As the Ecclesiastes writer so adequately puts it

> That's the whole story. Here now is my final conclusion: Fear God and obey his commands, for this is everyone's duty.

No grumbling and complaining about life

The unfairness of life

No getting angry with self

Life

God

Life is what it is

A battle!

I know these statements in regard to life are tough

They are even tougher when we ourselves are going through battles

How do you minister to someone who has lost a loved one?

A job

A home

A business

Doing battle with cancer

How do you minister to someone who has lost everything they may have owned?

Who has just lost their job

Their home

Going through bankruptcy

One who, because they have no place to stay, is living out of his or her car

Under a bridge

How do you minister to the wounded

Someone who just found out that they have stage four or five cancer

Laying on their death bed

Angry

Maybe even angry at God

How do you minister to the wounded

How do you minister to someone who has been abused almost all their lives

To someone who may have been physically or even sexually abused

Suffered emotional and psychological abuse all—or almost all—of their lives

When that abuse may have involved a family member or close friend

How do you minister to someone who is battling substance abuse

Drugs
Alcohol

How do you minister to the one who feels wounded?
Wounds
Real or imagined
Real or not
Wounds are real in the sense that they hurt
Cause us pain
How do we minister to the wounded?
Carefully and with lots of love
We may not have the answers—and chances are we won't
Sometimes, words are not necessary
Just our presence
Our show of love—our being there
We don't have to have the answers
God does!
And we should leave it at that
Angst
We relate to them the same way
Our response to them may be the same
They all hurt and ache the same
They can burden us down
Weigh us down the same
They can make us angry and bitter just the same

They can make us want to lash out at others
At God the same
Someone could have done me wrong
Or
I could think they had done me wrong
In my head
In my mind
I see it
It is real
Real to me
It doesn't matter
Either way
They feel the same
They hurt the same

We Have to Be Careful with Wounds

It's difficult to tell someone who is walking through difficulty that what they are feeling is not real
However, in this life, there are two things we go through
The battle
And the battles the battle produce
Our perceived wounds are, more often than not, simply the products
The effects of our battles
They are what the battle—and the battles—produce

The hurts

The pains

The wrongs

The injustices

The mistreatment and abuses

These are not the real wounds we experience or suffer in life

They are the attendants to life

The attendants to the battle

They come with life

To put it another way, they are the tests and opportunities of life

They come to try us

To provide us with an opportunity to rise above

And not allow what we may perceive as a wound to turn into a real one

Our experience in battle

Maturity is our goal in life

Spiritual maturity

However

Even the most mature believer

The Jobs of this life

Can and do struggle with the nature of life

We have to admit

Life is not easy

It is tough

And

It is tougher for some than others!

God's admonishment of Job is interesting

Void of what we may think of as real sympathy

Compassion

We say

Well, how come God is not sorry for all that Job has been through?

To God

An everlasting and righteous God

Job has overstepped the line

God was saying

Job

You need to understand who I am

Who you are

And the nature of life

God transcends life

He is above life

Yet He created life

Dictates and controls life

God is ultimately responsible for all that goes on in life!

> Then the LORD answered Job from the whirlwind: "Who is this that questions my wisdom with such ignorant words? Brace yourself like a man, because I have some questions for you, and you must answer them. "Where were you when I laid the foundations

of the earth? Tell me, if you know so much. Who determined its dimensions?" (Job 38:1-7).

Sometime later, and after God had put life into perspective

> Then the LORD said to Job, "Do you still want to argue with the Almighty? You are God's critic, but do you have the answers?"
>
> Then Job replied to the LORD, "I am nothing—how could I ever find the answers? I will cover my mouth with my hand. I have said too much already. I have nothing more to say" (Job 40:1-5).

Yes, when we are wounded

We can get angry and want to lash out at God

However

It behooves us

Once again

To heed the advice of the wisest man who ever lived

Solomon

> Here now is my final conclusion: Fear God and obey his commands, for this is everyone's duty. Nothing more; nothing less! (Ecclesiastes 12:13).

God was not unsympathetic towards Job

God turns around and blesses Job's life four times more than before

God was trying to teach Job a lesson about life

A most valuable lesson

It is the same lesson God is trying to teach us!
We who
Like Job
Servants of the Almighty, loving, gracious, and righteous God!

One final time
What we may perceive as a wound
Can cause us to become wounded
Can cause us to sin
We have to be careful with the "wounds"!
No
The real wounds are not what we experience in life
Not the things that happen to us
The real wounds are what our experiences
The things that happen to us
Produce on the inside of us
Again, the apostle James writes:

> "And remember, when you are being tempted, do not say, 'God is tempting me.' God is never tempted to do wrong, and he never tempts anyone else. Temptation comes from our own desires, which entice us and drag us away. These desires give birth to sinful actions. And when sin is allowed to grow, it gives birth to death" (James 1:13-15).

However, the Bible does speak of the involvement of the enemy

The role of the devil in our lives is also huge

It cannot be overestimated

It is a tragedy, or impending tragedy, to not believe in the devil

This is a boon for the devil

It says in 1 Peter:

"Stay alert! Watch out for your great enemy, the devil. He prowls around like a roaring lion, looking for someone to devour. Stand firm against him, and be strong in your faith" (1 Peter 5:8-9).

One of the enemy's roles is to pour salt on our wounds

Again, our wounds can be dangerous

Wounds have written all over them:

Fragile

Dangerous

Explosive

Handle with care!

This is essentially because wounds don't stay at one level

They burst out and become greater wounds

Wounds that turn into scars

Deadly and dangerous, the scars kill

We should minister to the "wounded"

We should avail ourselves of every opportunity to minister to the wounded

Yes

Of course, we are to minister to the wounded

Who better to minister to the wounded than the wounded

We are all, to some degree, walking, breathing, wounded souls

Again

The real wounds are not what happen to us

Again, they are products—and the by-products—of life

They are the potentially explosive seeds that can lead to real wounds taking shape and coming to life in our lives

We feel that someone has wronged us

Disrespected us

Abused us

Even if this were true

We still need to be careful how we react

A wound, real or imagined, can lead us down the path to sin

Again, it is not what happens to us in the heat of battle

In life

It is how we respond to what happens to us

CHAPTER 7

Cain's Battles, Wounds, and Scars

The Battle—and the battles—produce wounds

We have to understand this!

Wounds, we have said, tend to turn into scars

However, our wounds don't have to turn into scars

As we have stated, God has given us a measure of power and control over our lives

It is a gift from a loving and respectful God

It is the gift of choice

Something that we call free will

However, it is really more about power

Power and control

The two are synonymous

God is sovereign

He has ultimate control and power over everything

This is why we call Him King and Lord

The term King and Lord, among other things, conjure up the idea of owner

Lord really means owner

Or the owner

So God is all-powerful

God is loving

Caring

Full of wisdom

In His love and wisdom, God wanted us to experience life as He experiences life

God wanted us to have a taste of His sovereign power

God wanted us to be in charge of a slice of life

The earth

And all that live upon the earth

The Bible says in Psalms:

> The heavens belong to the LORD, but he has given the earth to all humanity (humans) (Psalm 115:16, parenthetical mine).
>
> When I look at the night sky and see the work of your fingers—the moon and the stars you set in place—what are mere mortals that you should think about them, human beings that you should care for them? Yet you made them only a little lower than God and crowned them with glory and honor. You gave them charge of everything you made, putting all things under their authority—the flocks and the herds and all the wild animals, the birds in the sky, the fish in

the sea. And everything that swims the ocean currents (Psalm 8:5-8).

We can go back—as we should—to almost the beginning of time

Right after life was turned into a battle

The story of Cain and Abel is no mere story

It is life

It shows the nature of life

The battle

And the battles produced by the battle and in the midst of the battle

The story of Cain and Abel is also about wounds—real and imagined

Wounds that we perceived as wounds

And real

Deeply spiritual wounds

The story of Cain and Abel is also about how wounds can so easily turn into scars

The story of Cain and Abel is full of battles

First, we have the battle that is life

Then, the battles that go on in life

That are a part of life

In addition

There must have been battles that must have been a part of Cain's—if not Abel's—thinking

What do I give to God?

What is the right amount?

What does the Word of God say?

Should I trust the Word of God?

Will God charge me if I don't?

Cain must have wrangled, or at least rolled it over in his mind, exactly what and how much to give to God

Even our thoughts and our decisions could be a part of the struggle

The battle

Then, when God rejected Cain's offering, Cain must have really struggled with how to respond

Cain must have said to himself

This is not right

God has done me wrong

An injustice

How do I get justice for myself?

How do I get even?

What should I do?

Which path should I take?

Should I try to get even with God?

Or do I take it out on my brother—who I can see—and whom God has chosen over me

These are all signs, indications of battles

Mostly, battles going on in Cain's mind

Battles of the mind!

Our Wounds Reveal a Lack of Faith

Then there is the battle to believe that are present in the life of Cain

Underlying Cain's less-than-satisfactory gift was a lack of faith in God

Obedience to God

Trust in God

Even today, many of us still struggle over the concept and act of the tithing

All of these were battles confronting Cain and Abel

Abel chose to obey God, show his love for God

The Bible is clear:

> Loving God means keeping his commandments, and his commandments are not burdensome (1 John 5:3).

Our consciences bear evidence of the truth of God's Word

So Abel loved God by honoring His Word

Cain, on the other hand, in wrestling with his own conscience, decided to disobey God

The wounds that Cain suffered in his battle were

Anger

Bitterness

Resentment

And jealousy

The perceived wound that Cain felt—which was not a wound, but life—part of the injustices of life

It could be our own unjust ways

Our sinful ways

The real wounds—

The anger

The bitterness

The hatred and resentment toward his brother

The quiet rage

The jealousy

Would all turn into a deep-down, deep-seated wound that Cain allowed to linger

Fester and grow

That would eventually turn into a scar

It is important to note that Cain's decisions and actions were of his own doing

His choice

God didn't have anything to do with Cain's choice

The devil didn't make Cain do it!

Cain did it of his own volition

Interestingly, Cain used the same gift that God gives to all of us

The gift of choice

The gift God, a loving and respectful God, gives

Even if we choose to go against Him

Love, we say, is unconditional

Love makes itself vulnerable

Wounds are like weights
They weigh us down
They cause us pain, uncomfortableness, irritability
They can even affect our demeanor and looks
The Bible suggests that the inner struggle
Battle
War going on inside of Cain became visible on the outside
It made him look "dejected"

Our Wounds Can Affect Our Choices

Life is a matter of choice
The choices and the decisions we make
Life is also about how we respond to the battles and the wounds we suffer in battles
As we have been saying—which is also true in the case of Cain and Abel—we live our lives at the intersection of our battles and our wounds
This is an all-important place for us because it brings us to that moment of decision
It is an important place for God because it lets Him see the level of our faith
Our character
This is where God meets us

> When it was time for the harvest, Cain presented some of his crops as a gift to the Lord. Abel also brought a gift—the best portions of the firstborn

lambs from his flock. The Lord accepted Abel and his gift (Genesis 4:3-4).

Cain, in effect, allowed his wounds to turn into a scar
This is quite apparent from the conversation God has with Cain

> "Why are you so angry?" the Lord asked Cain. "Why do you look so dejected? You will be accepted if you do what is right. But if you refuse to do what is right, then watch out! Sin is crouching at the door, eager to control you. But you must subdue it and be its master" (Genesis 4:6-7).

Our wounds—the scars—oftentimes protrude from our inner selves to our outer

> One day Cain suggested to his brother, 'Let's go out into the fields.' And while they were in the field, Cain attacked his brother, Abel, and killed him (Genesis 4:8).

Our wounds, when they turn into scars, can be harmful
They can cause us to worry
To brood
They can make us sick
Physically
Emotionally
Psychologically
And spiritually
They can fill us with anger

Cause us to lash out

> "Afterward the Lord asked Cain, 'Where is your brother? Where is Abel?'
>
> 'I don't know,' Cain responded. 'Am I my brother's guardian?'" (Genesis 4:9)

The scars, as they begin to set in, can and do impede our spiritual "walk" with God

The wounds can take up our time, like an obsession

They can prevent us from leading productive lives

They can rob us of our God-given purpose and potential

They can derail us

Cause us to lose control

And to spiral completely out of control after venturing out onto that slippery slope of life

Without intervention, the wounds can and do lead to death and destruction

Much death and destruction

Our own death and destruction, physically and spiritually

Our Wounds Can Rob Us of Our Purpose

Cain was a farmer

His job was to till the stubborn soil

Made stubborn when life got turned into a struggle

A battle

This was his purpose in life

A life without purpose is a life removed from the safety, protection, power, and presence of God

A life left to its own devices

A life left to its own devices is a life that is ruled by a spirit other than God's

Could be our own spirit

Or an evil spirit

For all intent and purpose, they are the same

We know that the Holy Spirit produces this kind of fruit in our lives

Love

Joy

Peace

Patience

Kindness

Goodness

Faithfulness

Gentleness

And self-control

And we know this to be true of a human heart/spirit

"The human heart is the most deceitful of all things, and desperately wicked. Who really knows how bad it is?" (Jeremiah 17:9).

It goes on to say:

> "But I, the Lord, search all hearts and examine secret motives. I give all people their due rewards, according to what their actions deserve" (Jeremiah 17:10).

Again:

> "Afterward the Lord asked Cain, 'Where is your brother? Where is Abel?' 'I don't know,' Cain responded. 'Am I my brother's guardian?' (Genesis 4:9).

Another version of the Bible reads:

> "Am I my brother's keeper?"

Highlights even more so the anger that Cain felt in this situation

> "But the Lord said, 'What have you done? Listen! Your brother's blood cries out to me from the ground! Now you are cursed and banished from the ground, which has swallowed your brother's blood. No longer will the ground yield good crops for you, no matter how hard you work! From now on you will be a homeless wanderer on the earth.' Cain replied to the Lord, 'My punishment is too great for me to bear! You have banished me from the land and from your presence; you have made me a homeless wanderer. Anyone who finds me will kill me!' (Genesis 4:10-14).

Finally

We find—and reveal, or live out—our purpose in the presence of God

As we have been saying, the scars can take control of our lives

Make us sick

Rob us of our peace

Our joy

The scars take over our lives

Control us

Cause us to lose control

The scars can also rob us of our productivity

And most importantly, the scars can rob us of our God-given potential and purpose

Bereft of purpose, we are, for all intent and purpose, dead

CHAPTER 8

Joseph—The Key to Our Battles Is Preparation

Joseph was prepared for battle
This is the one outstanding truth about Joseph's life
This is not to say that Joseph was a perfect human being
That he could not fail
Joseph was one of us
Like any of us
Except for the grace of God
and Joseph's response to God's grace
We are saying that, Joseph, armed with the Word of God
Successfully went through the battles
Endured some of the "slings and arrows" of this life
But did not succumb to the wounds—the scars of this life

God lifts up certain ones to be His servants

His chosen man or woman

His chosen people

Along with His presence, He gives them His Word

The relationship that God establishes with His chosen ones is centered around His Word

Can we commit to follow Him and His Word?

Can we remain loyal to Him?

Obedient

God Prepares Us for the Battles

This is God preparing us for battle

God even chooses to call them His messengers, friends, and servants

God blesses them with His presence

His love

God chooses a time and place to test those He has chosen and called

It is important to God that we are tested

That we past the test

Blessing is always in the offing after the testing

But in the moment of His choosing

God wants to see how we will respond

How we will put to use one of the most wonderful and precious gift that He has given to us

This power to choose for ourselves!

Again

We call it free will

This power to choose is one that God chooses not to interfere with

This power to choose for ourselves will establish in front of God whether we have His kind of character

Faith

Faith in Him!

God frees us

He frees us to see whether we will go with Him or against Him?

Will we choose to go His way or our own way?

follow Him or follow self

When tested, Cain decided to go his own way

To follow self

This is one of the most common egregious errors we tend to make in life

The Bible tells us clearly

It says:

"Lean not unto thine own understanding" (Proverbs 3:5, KJV)

This is very dangerous

It is like a ship traveling at night and deciding to ignore the light of the lighthouse

Jesus said

When under the greatest strain of His life

When going through His most intense battle:
Father, not my will be done, but yours!

Self
Self means our own all-too-human emotions and desires
It is reliance on our own feelings
Thoughts
Philosophy and wisdom
God knows who we are
The "stuff" we are made of
It is He who has put them there, on the inside of us
He uses it all for His purpose and glory
If He has put it there, then it is sufficient to take us through the battles
We have all we need to meet with success, victory, and triumph in the battle and the battles that flow from life
In other words, God has fully equipped us to go through the battles while not incurring the scars

God Keeps His Promises through the Battles

Joseph was prepared for the battles he would face in life
God raised up Joseph for the purpose of testing and modeling

The Bible says:

> "Until the time came to fulfill his dreams, the LORD tested Joseph's character" (Psalm 105:19).

The hallmark of Joseph's life was his obedience

Joseph is a prefiguring and a foreshadowing of Christ

As we go through our battles, it behooves us to remember

Recall

Reminisce

Reflect on

This is how we remain steady

It is important for us to remember what we saw when God first called us

What we saw of God

His revelations

His revelations of Himself that contain His promises

Promises for us

God's promises never fail

They are real

They are indestructible

They will come to pass

We want to hold firmly to the promises of God

The infallible Word of God

The promises of God will keep us

Carry us

Fortify us
Sustain us

Joseph's early battles came in the form of his brothers
They hated Joseph
They were jealous of him
They plotted to take his life

> "When Joseph's brothers saw him coming, they recognized him in the distance. As he approached, they made plans to kill him. 'Here comes the dreamer!' they said. 'Come on, let's kill him and throw him into one of these cisterns. We can tell our father, "A wild animal has eaten him." Then we'll see what becomes of his dreams!'" (Genesis 37:18-20).

When We Are Tested
It is always a good idea to reflect
Reflect on what we saw when we were a young Christian
Just setting out on our walk with God
What did God reveal to us?
What did God show us?
What was the vision or the dream?

So, at the first opportunity they had, Joseph's brothers tried to get rid of Joseph
They threw him into a pit
A cistern
This was not easy

Our battles never are

Dark

Maybe damp and wet

Crawling with insects, bugs, and reptiles

Starvation looming

Joseph didn't give in

Give up

He trusted God

When tested

Joseph must have said to himself, "This is not what I saw in any of the dreams!"

Later, his brothers sold him into slavery

His battles had just begun

His hands and feet were shackled

A shackle around his neck so that he would be dragged behind the caravan of traders riding on camels

This was the nature of being sold into slavery

This was the nature of Joseph's battle

Through the hot, thirsty desert

The heat and the cold

The intense heat

The wind

And the windstorms

The darkness

The dust

And the dust storms
The strange, creepy, crawly creatures
Deadly desert scorpions
Snakes
Lizards
Fear
Afraid for his life
We are no strangers to this kind of fear
Yet
Joseph didn't give in
Give up
He trusted God
Joseph must have said to himself
When tested
"This is not what I saw"

Sold into slavery
Into Potiphar's household
Through the battles
We hear these words
They flash on the pages of our Bibles
Between the lines
"But God was with Joseph"

> When Joseph was taken to Egypt by the Ishmaelite traders, he was purchased by Potiphar, an Egyptian officer. Potiphar was captain of the guard for

Pharaoh, the king of Egypt. The LORD was with Joseph, so he succeeded in everything he did as he served in the home of his Egyptian master. Potiphar noticed this and realized that the LORD was with Joseph, giving him success in everything he did. This pleased Potiphar, so he soon made Joseph his personal attendant. He put him in charge of his entire household and everything he owned. From the day Joseph was put in charge of his master's household and property, the LORD began to bless Potiphar's household for Joseph's sake. All his household affairs ran smoothly, and his crops and livestock flourished. So Potiphar gave Joseph complete administrative responsibility over everything he owned. With Joseph there, he didn't worry about a thing—except what kind of food to eat! (Genesis 39:1-6)

God's promises are real

They always come to pass

For instance, God had told Abraham

That his descendants will certainly go down into Egypt

They will suffer

They will be cast into bondage

Slavery

But that He, God, would be with them

He would go with them through the battles

If you were called by God

If God showed Himself to you

Through His Word

The sharing of His Word

In a dream
In a perpetually burning bush
Whatever the form
Then you must ask yourself, "What was the revelation?"
The vision I saw
That dream I had
What did I see?
I am talking directly to you
What did you see?
Cancer?
If not, it is the plot of the enemy
It's gone as far as God is concerned
Hypertension?
Diabetes?
Loss of sight?
Ability to walk?
Depression?
Crippling financial hardships?
Overwhelming family challenges or crises?
These, too, are the works of the enemy
When we are tested
It helps to recall, reflect
What did I see when God first called me?
When He saved me

What did you see when God called you?

If what you are going through is not what you saw when God first called you, then don't worry

Circumstances are circumstances

Temporary

They are never permanent fixtures in our lives

Nor should we see them as such

We can rise above our circumstances in life

We just need to stay focused

Stay focused on God

Don't ever be blinded by your current circumstance or circumstances

The same one who called you is also the one who is in control

The Battles Will Test Us

Potiphar's wife lied on Joseph:

> Joseph was a very handsome and well-built young man, and Potiphar's wife soon began to look at him lustfully. 'Come and sleep with me,' she demanded. But Joseph refused. 'Look,' he told her. 'My master trusts me with everything in his entire household. No one here has more authority than I do. He has held back nothing from me except you, because you are his wife. How could I do such a wicked thing? It would be a great sin against God.' She kept putting pressure on Joseph day after day, but he refused to sleep with her, and he kept out of her way as much as possible.

> One day, however, no one else was around when he went in to do his work. She came and grabbed him by his cloak, demanding, 'Come on, sleep with me!' Joseph tore himself away, but he left his cloak in her hand as he ran from the house (Genesis 39:6-12).

Joseph knew the Word

The Bible says to flee from even the appearance of evil

Even if it means leaving your clothes behind

Even if it means ruining your little bit of pride and dignity

> When she saw that she was holding his cloak and he had fled, she called out to her servants. Soon all the men came running. 'Look!' she said. 'My husband has brought this Hebrew slave here to make fools of us! He came into my room to rape me, but I screamed. When he heard me scream, he ran outside and got away, but he left his cloak behind with me. She kept the cloak with her until her husband came home. Then she told him her story. 'That Hebrew slave you've brought into our house tried to come in and fool around with me,' she said. 'But when I screamed, he ran outside, leaving his cloak with me!' Potiphar was furious when he heard his wife's story about how Joseph had treated her. So he took Joseph and threw him into the prison where the king's prisoners were held, and there he remained (Genesis 39:13-20).

God Blesses Joseph through His Battles

His battle continued

Yet again, those words flashed up on the screen

Between the pages

To encourage us

"But the Lord was with Joseph!"

> "But the LORD was with Joseph in the prison and showed him his faithful love. And the LORD made Joseph a favorite with the prison warden. Before long, the warden put Joseph in charge of all the other prisoners and over everything that happened in the prison. The warden had no more worries, because Joseph took care of everything. The LORD was with him and caused everything he did to succeed" (Genesis 39:21-23).

Joseph did not spend his time worrying

Like some of us would be wont to do

Nor did he sit there and pitch a pity party

Joseph simply took over the prison

Well, God, through Joseph, took over the prison

Joseph was empowered

When tested

Joseph must have comforted himself with the thought

"This is not what I saw!"

Like Jesus of Nazareth was empowered by God, the Holy Spirit

In the midst of His battle

When we are chosen

When we are called and appointed

When we are blessed

And
When we go through battles

When we go through battles
In the name of the Lord
A couple of things happen
One, we experience success
Victory
Victory over our circumstances
Triumph
When we go through battles
It's as if we are stamped
(And we are)
Sealed
Shielded and protected
The property of our God and Savior
Our Lord
Our Creator
The Creator of everything
The heavens
The Earth
And all that is within them
The whole entire universe
Others can see God in us
Potiphar saw God in Joseph

The prison warden saw God in Joseph
Pharoah said
It is quite obvious that you are endowed by God
Some may want to debate this and or that
For you and me, it must be settled
Then
When we go through battles
Endurance will always breed success
Victory
Victory over our circumstances
Triumph
Our promotion
Our battles, though tests, also afford us opportunities created and ordained by God
God, through Joseph, interpreted Pharaoh's dream
The Egyptians now knew—truly knew—who Joseph was
You cannot deny
Overlook
True success
You cannot deny the hand of God on events unfolding
God even gave Pharaoh a vision!
Pharaoh embraced the triumphant moment
The wisdom that flowed through and from God
Pharaoh thought it was him who promoted Joseph that day
It didn't matter

All that mattered was that the glory of God and His Word were exalted

> So Pharaoh asked his officials, "Can we find anyone else like this man so obviously filled with the spirit of God?" Then Pharaoh said to Joseph, "Since God has revealed the meaning of the dreams to you, clearly no one else is as intelligent or wise as you are, you will be in charge of my court, and all my people will take orders from you. Only I, sitting on my throne, will have a rank higher than yours." Pharaoh said to Joseph, "I hereby put you in charge of the entire land of Egypt." Then Pharaoh removed his signet ring from his hand and placed it on Joseph's finger. He dressed him in fine linen clothing and hung a gold chain around his neck. Then he had Joseph ride in the chariot reserved for his second-in-command. And wherever Joseph went, the command was shouted, "Kneel down!" So Pharaoh put Joseph in charge of all Egypt. And Pharaoh said to him, "I am Pharaoh, but no one will lift a hand or foot in the entire land of Egypt without your approval" (Genesis 41:38-44).

We are called, like Joseph, to go through the battles
In Joseph, we see the antithesis of the wounds
The complete absence of the wounds/scars
Anger
Hate
Bitterness
Resentment
Jealousy
Revenge

Unforgiveness

No pride

Greed

Covetousness

No holding on to grudges

All we see is

Just love

Pure, unadulterated love

Love and forgiveness

Forgiveness

That special part of God's love

That very special part of God's love that draws us closer to God

Connects us to God like a bridge

Brings us into agreement, oneness, with God

As life was ordained to be

> The waiters served Joseph at his own table, and his brothers were served at a separate table. Joseph told each of his brothers where to sit, and to their amazement, he seated them according to age, from oldest to youngest. And Joseph filled their plates with food from his own table, giving Benjamin five times as much as he gave the others. So they feasted and drank freely with him (Genesis 43:32-34).

And

> But Joseph replied, "Don't be afraid of me. Am I God, that I can punish you? You intended to harm me,

but God intended it all for good. He brought me to this position so I could save the lives of many people (Genesis 50:19-20).

Revelation

Purpose

It always comes back to these

Faith comes through revelation

Seeing the revelation

Believing it

Thinking and reflecting on it

Discerning it

Praying and asking God to help us, give us greater and deeper insight

Purpose

Understanding it

Walking in God's purpose for our lives always brings peace, freedom, joy, and love

Love covers a multitude of sins

Love

The opposite of hate

A mysterious force

Not in and of ourselves

Not coming from us

Not something we are capable of mounting

Love

Love and forgiveness

Will always allow us to go through the battles without the scars

God wants to go with us into battles

When we call out to Him

When we humble ourselves and submit ourselves to Him

When we agree to obey and live according to His every word

God can—and wants to—heal all our "wounds"

Bandage them up

Pour soothing balm and anointment

Mysteriously

On our "wounds"

Like the good Samaritan on the treacherous road to Jericho

God's mission in life is to always bring us successfully through our battles

Joseph said to his brothers after many years of separation:

> "Don't be afraid of me. Am I God, that I can punish you? You intended to harm me, but God intended it all for good. He brought me to this position so I could save the lives of many people! (Genesis 50:19-20).

CHAPTER 9

Saul's Battles, Wounds, and Scars—The Tragic and Lonely Demise of a King

Life can be a lonely experience or existence

Especially when we turn our backs on God

Reject him

Spurn His love

Choose to go our way instead of His

It is also a foolish idea

It is a foolish idea because we are rejecting the love of God

His love

His presence/power

And His protection

His presence is where we discover and live out God's purpose for our lives

It is where we find peace

Happiness

Joy

And success

Moses clearly understood this:

> Then Moses said, "If you don't personally go with us, don't make us leave this place. How will anyone know that you look favorably on me—on me and on your people—if you don't go with us? For your presence among us sets your people and me apart from all other people on the earth" (Exodus 33:15-16).

David understood the importance of God's presence

> Oh, give me back my joy again; you have broken me—now let me rejoice. Don't keep looking at my sins. Remove the stain of my guilt. Create in me a clean heart, O God. Renew a loyal spirit within me. Do not banish me from your presence, and don't take your Holy Spirit from me (Psalms 51:8).

The people wanted a king

Saul was Israel's first king

Saul rose to prominence as a result of the people of Israel demanding a human king

Before Saul, God, Himself, was Israel's king

It was God's desire to rule over His people, bless them, and to have them prosper in the new land that He had promised their ancestors, Abraham, Isaac, and Jacob

However, the people kept insisting on having a king

They wanted a human king to rule over them like the other nations around them

God, through the prophet Samuel, told them that this was a bad idea

That a human king would rule over them oppressively

But the people insisted

As we have been saying all along, God is a loving and wise God

He loves us

And He cares for us

However, He is also a respectful God

He has given us a measure of power and control over our lives

God has given us this taste of power and control over our lives, even though it comes with vulnerability—for Him

The Battle for Our Hearts

We can choose to either choose or reject God

Love

True love is vulnerable

It involves vulnerability

It's unconditional

This is what makes love, love

God desire for us humans is for us to choose Him

This reflects the nature of God's love

God gives us this slice of power and control, even though we may choose to go against Him

As was the case, here, with the Children of Israel desiring a king

God had warned them that a human king would come up short

Would be found to be wanting

Lacking

God warned the people that a human being ruling over them would be disastrous

God alone is that perfect, benevolent King

The One who loves us, cares for us, and wants what is best for us

> All the elders of Israel met at Ramah to discuss the matter with Samuel. "Look," they told him, "you are now old, and your sons are not like you. Give us a king to judge us like all the other nations have." Samuel was displeased with their request and went to the LORD for guidance. "Do everything they say to you," the LORD replied, "for they are rejecting me, not you. They don't want me to be their king any longer. Ever since I brought them from Egypt they have continually abandoned me and followed other gods. And now they are giving you the same treatment. Do as they ask, but solemnly warn them about the way a king will reign over them." So Samuel passed on the LORD's warning to the people who were asking him for a king (1 Samuel 8:4-10).
>
> But the people refused to listen to Samuel's warning. "Even so, we still want a king," they said. "We want to be like the nations around us. Our king will judge us and lead us into battle." So Samuel repeated to the

LORD what the people had said, and the LORD replied, "Do as they say, and give them a king." Then Samuel agreed and sent the people home (1 Samuel 8:19-22).

Saul's great battle

Saul's greatest battle

Was a lack of faith

I believe that there are two levels of faith

Faith, I believe, can be just simply believing

Believing in oneself

Having confidence

Jesus said:

> "Don't be afraid. Just have faith" (Mark 5:36).

Then there is faith in God

Which is also inclusive of faith in Jesus

Which is the highest level and represents, from a believer's viewpoint, true faith

So Jesus said:

> Don't let your hearts be troubled. Trust in God, and trust also in me (John 14:1).

Saul, we see from early on in his life

Lacked faith on all levels

Saul

Not only doubted himself, but he felt that he was inadequate
Saul suffered from an inferiority complex
He felt he was unworthy to be king
Even after God had told Samuel to anoint him
Because he doubted
Because he allowed self to get in the way
Saul lacked confidence
Confidence in himself
And confidence in God

The Battle to Trust and Obey God

Israel was God's chosen people
Faith in God
Obedience to God was the requirement for their success
This did not change with the anointing of a king
As a matter of fact, strict obedience to God was expected of both the people and whoever the king was
God's demand for the king
In this critical area of life
Exemplifying faith in God
Was for the king to lead by example
It was in this area
Faith in God
Hearkening to the voice of God

Believing God

Relying on God

Relying solely on God

Being obedient to God and His Word

Honoring God

Loving God

It was in this area of his life that Saul proved himself to be an abject failure

Saul committed a cardinal sin—as far as God is concerned

Saul disregarded the Word of God

He took matters into his own hands

Saul Walks—stumbles—into Destiny

Destiny is not a given

Oftentimes, we do not know the "why"

The why for our existence

Why we were born

Why we have embarked on this or that journey

Why our parents gave us birth

Sometimes

On our journeys

We get lost

Sometimes, we can become hopelessly lost

However

Our purpose is not lost to God

And where we may be fumbling and bumbling our way through life

God might be leading us to our purpose

Our destiny

If you think I sound like an expert in this area of fumbling and bumbling through life

It is because I am

That is, before God took ahold of my life

Spun me around

Turned me in the direction that he wanted me to go in

The direction of His plan and purpose for my life!

God holds the key to our destiny

> One day Kish's donkeys strayed away, and he told Saul, "Take a servant with you, and go look for the donkeys." Finally, they entered the region of Zuph, and Saul said to his servant, "Let's go home. By now my father will be more worried about us than about the donkeys!" But the servant said, "I've just thought of something! There is a man of God who lives here in this town. He is held in high honor by all the people because everything he says comes true. Let's go find him. Perhaps he can tell us which way to go" (1 Samuel 9:3-6).

Obviously, Saul—and his companion—did not have a clue about the real purpose and nature of their mission

Their journey

As far as they were concerned

They were on a mission to find a donkey
But God had other plans
It is God
All God
Who puts us in a direct collision path with our destiny

> So they entered the town, and as they passed through the gates, Samuel was coming out toward them to go up to the place of worship. Now the LORD had told Samuel the previous day, "About this time tomorrow I will send you a man from the land of Benjamin. Anoint him to be the leader of my people, Israel. Just then Saul approached Samuel at the gateway and asked, "Can you please tell me where the seer's house is?" "I am the seer!" Samuel replied. "Go up to the place of worship ahead of me. We will eat there together, and in the morning I'll tell you what you want to know and send you on your way. And don't worry about those donkeys that were lost three days ago, for they have been found. And I am here to tell you that you and your family are the focus of all Israel's hopes." Saul replied, "But I'm only from the tribe of Benjamin, the smallest tribe in Israel, and my family is the least important of all the families of that tribe! Why are you talking like this to me?" (1 Samuel 9:14-21).

Oftentimes
What we think our mission is all about
Our purpose in life
Can have very little to do with our real purpose
It can be just a means to move us in the direction of purpose

> Then Samuel took a flask of olive oil and poured it over Saul's head. He kissed Saul and said, "I am doing this because the LORD has appointed you to be the ruler over Israel, his special possession" (1 Samuel 10:1).

> So Samuel brought all the tribes of Israel before the LORD, and the tribe of Benjamin was chosen by lot. Then he brought each family of the tribe of Benjamin before the LORD, and the family of the Matrites was chosen. And finally Saul son of Kish was chosen from among them. But when they looked for him, he had disappeared! So they asked the LORD, "Where is he?" And the LORD replied, "He is hiding among the baggage" (1 Samuel 10:20-22).

Immediately, we see something amiss with Saul

A chink in his armor

Life

Character

Saul hides

Shrinks away from responsibility

Even though

God

Through Samuel

Just finished saying to him

"The LORD has appointed you to be the ruler over Israel, his special possession."

Saul's earliest battle, then, is in the area of faith

Faith in himself

And faith in God

We would say

Brother Saul is not getting off to a good start at all!

The challenge to believe God

Rely on God

Be obedient to God

Would also lead to the critical wound and scar that would plague Saul for the rest of his life

Remember, a wound oftentimes stems from a feeling of having been wronged

Slighted

Overlooked

Hurt

Injured

Done an injustice

Abused

Mistreated

Demoted

Fired

And so on

The demotions and the firing are not the real wounds

They might be symptomatic

The cause

Or the trigger

But they are never the real wounds!

Saul's real wounds would come later

The wound that would rise up in him

Take root

Turn into a scar

That would take over Saul's life

Cause him to lose control

And eventually spiral completely out of control

The real wounds are what the feeling of being wronged produces in us

They may produce

Anger

Hatred

Bitterness

Resentment

Jealousy

A desire for revenge

A spirit of unforgiveness

The Bible records the onset of the "wounds" in Saul's life

The lead-up to his real wounds

The wounds of anger

Bitter hatred and jealousy toward David, the new king

The king in the offing

The king-in-waiting

By the way, fear

Irrational fear is also a battle

Stemming from the battle

It, too, can become a wound
As far as God is concerned

Saul was now king
Samuel was the prophet
And war was being waged between Israel and its arch-enemy, the Philistines

> Meanwhile, Saul stayed at Gilgal, and his men were trembling with fear. Saul waited there seven days for Samuel, as Samuel had instructed him earlier, but Samuel still didn't come. Saul realized that his troops were rapidly slipping away. So he demanded, "Bring me the burnt offering and the peace offerings!" And Saul sacrificed the burnt offering himself (1 Samuel 13:7-9).

Samuel was the prophet
The messenger of God
The very Word of God
Saul's ongoing battle with faith
Would surface again when he was told by Samuel to wait before going into battle
In other words
Not take matters into his own hands
Saul did just the opposite
Disregarding the Word of God
Not a good way to go into battle
The battle going on in Saul's life was a battle of faith
Trusting God

Trusting His Word

Saul is no different from many of us

Like Abraham and Sarah

God gives His Word

After a while, we feel that God is taking too long

We grow impatient

We take matters into our own hands

It belies our lack of trust in God

Our obedience to God and His Word

Our faith in God

> Just as Saul was finishing with the burnt offering, Samuel arrived. Saul went out to meet and welcome him, but Samuel said, "What is this you have done?" Saul replied, "I saw my men scattering from me, and you didn't arrive when you said you would, and the Philistines are at Micmash ready for battle. So I said
>
> 'The Philistines are ready to march against us at Gilgal, and I haven't even asked for the LORD's help!' So I felt compelled to offer the burnt offering myself before you came." "How foolish!" Samuel exclaimed. "You have not kept the command the LORD your God gave you. Had you kept it, the LORD would have established your kingdom over Israel forever. But now your kingdom must end, for the LORD has sought out a man after his own heart. The LORD has already appointed him to be the leader of his people, because you have not kept the LORD's command" (1 Samuel 13:10-14).

"How foolish," said Samuel

His words are instructive for us, as well
How foolish to go into battle without God
God abandons us when we abandon Him

> One day Samuel said to Saul, "It was the LORD who told me to anoint you as king of his people, Israel. Now listen to this message from the LORD! This is what the LORD of Heaven's Armies has declared: I have decided to settle accounts with the nation of Amalek for opposing Israel when they came from Egypt. Now go and completely destroy the entire Amalekite nation—men, women, children, babies, cattle, sheep, goats, camels, and donkeys" (1 Samuel 15:1-3).

Once again, God decides to test Saul through His Word

> Then Saul slaughtered the Amalekites from Havilah all the way to Shur, east of Egypt. He captured Agag, the Amalekite king, but completely destroyed everyone else. Saul and his men spared Agag's life and kept the best of the sheep and goats, the cattle, the fat calves, and the lambs—everything, in fact, that appealed to them. They destroyed only what was worthless or of poor quality (1 Samuel 15:7-9).

And once again, Saul fails
God sees our failure to follow his instructions as dishonoring Him
As disloyalty to Him

> Then the LORD said to Samuel, "I am sorry that I ever made Saul king, for he has not been loyal to me and has refused to obey my command." Samuel was so

deeply moved when he heard this that he cried out to the LORD all night. Early the next morning Samuel went to find Saul. Someone told him, "Saul went to the town of Carmel to set up a monument to himself; then he went on to Gilgal."

When Samuel finally found him, Saul greeted him cheerfully. "May the LORD bless you," he said. "I have carried out the LORD's command!"

"Then what is all the bleating of sheep and goats and the lowing of cattle I hear?" Samuel demanded.

"It's true that the army spared the best of the sheep, goats, and cattle," Saul admitted. "But they are going to sacrifice them to the LORD your God. We have destroyed everything else."

Then Samuel said to Saul, "Stop! Listen to what the LORD told me last night!"

"What did he tell you?" Saul asked.

And Samuel told him, "Although you may think little of yourself, are you not the leader of the tribes of Israel? The LORD has anointed you king of Israel. And the LORD sent you on a mission and told you, 'Go and completely destroy the sinners, the Amalekites, until they are all dead.' Why haven't you obeyed the LORD?

Why did you rush for the plunder and do what was evil in the LORD's sight?"

Saul has many shortcomings
Samuel points to one of them
A lack of self-confidence
Belief in himself

The key to a successful life

In other words

What takes us through the battle—and the battles of this life?

Our surrender!

Our complete surrender to God and His Word!

Our complete obedience to God

We must surrender our lives to the Word of God

It is because of God's Word that we have the Spirit of God

The Spirit also inhabits the Word

It is because of Jesus that we have the power, the presence of God in our lives living on the inside of us

That is, those of us who know God

Truly know Him

It is because of the eternal Word of God

The Word—the selfsame Word—that was in the beginning

With God

And who was God

The Word through whom all things were created

The same Word that came down to earth and dwell among us

Who we, humans, beheld His glory

True nature

His true nature—full of unfailing love and faithfulness

This Word

The one and only Son of God who was sent by God to give eternal life to all who believed in Him

This Word is why we have God's Holy Spirit to lead, guide, and direct us into battles

This is no trivial matter!

It's not some made up story

Some myth

Laugh and balk if you like

But this is God at work

What He promised a long time ago through the prophets in the Holy Scriptures

This is the nature of life—a life with God!

The battle is His

The battle—and the battles produced by and in life—all belong to Him

God simply commands us to get our lives in order

Then watch Him, allow Him, to go to work on our behalf!

All praise and thanks be to God for what He has done and continues to do in the lives of His people!

In fact, God values our obedience above all else

Even our good intentions

The sacrifices we say we are making to Him

> "But I did obey the LORD," Saul insisted. "I carried out the mission he gave me. I brought back King Agag, but I destroyed everyone else. Then my troops brought in the best of the sheep, goats, cattle, and plunder to sacrifice to the LORD your God in Gilgal."

> But Samuel replied, "What is more pleasing to the LORD: your burnt offerings and sacrifices or your obedience to his voice? Listen! Obedience is better than sacrifice, and submission is better than offering the fat of rams. Rebellion is as sinful as witchcraft, and stubbornness as bad as worshiping idols. So because you have rejected the command of the LORD, he has rejected you as king."

Our wounds are sins

Our lack of faith is a most grievous wound

A sin

> Then Saul admitted to Samuel, "Yes, I have sinned. I have disobeyed your instructions and the LORD's command, for I was afraid of the people and did what they demanded. But now, please forgive my sin and come back with me so that I may worship the LORD."
>
> But Samuel replied, "I will not go back with you! Since you have rejected the LORD's command, he has rejected you as king of Israel."

One of Saul's other wounds is put on display

His anger

Impatience

His impulsiveness

> As Samuel turned to go, Saul tried to hold him back and tore the hem of his robe. And Samuel said to him, "The LORD has torn the kingdom of Israel from you today and has given it to someone else— one who is better than you. And he who is the Glory of Israel will not lie, nor will he change his mind, for he is not

human that he should change his mind!" (1 Samuel 15:7-29).

We cannot overlook another important factor—the most important one—at play in Saul's life

And that is the will of God

With the anointing of David, the question arises

How free was Saul?

How free was he to change

Redirect

Do what was right

Saul

At any point in time was free to do the right thing

It's just that God knows us

He is a God who sees the end from the beginning

And while He doesn't control us, He knows us

And

Like Pharaoh

Whose stubborn heart led to God using Pharaoh's own stubborn heart to accomplish His will

(The Bible says God hardened the heart of Pharaoh's heart)

Here, too, with Saul

God would allow Saul's lack of faith

His fatal flaw

To accomplish His (God's perfect will)

Similar to the case of Pharaoh

It gets to a point where God's Spirit refuses to contend any longer with the human spirit

Precisely because of the sinful nature

The flaws of that human being

God knew that Saul would implode, so to speak

God knows our hearts

That is not to say that God caused Saul to sin

Rejected him because He had David in mind

However

Knowing the end from the beginning

God always has a plan

When humans fail

God always has a plan

God doesn't fail

Humans fail

And God always has a plan just in case humans decide to use their own free will to go against him

The Bible says

Before the creation of the world, the Lamb was slain

So Saul abandoned God

So God abandoned Saul

> Now the Spirit of the LORD had left Saul, and the LORD sent a tormenting spirit that filled him with depression and fear. Some of Saul's servants said to him, "A tormenting spirit from God is troubling you. Let us find a good musician to play the harp whenever

the tormenting spirit troubles you. He will play soothing music, and you will soon be well again."

"All right," Saul said. "Find me someone who plays well, and bring him here."

One of the servants said to Saul, "One of Jesse's sons from Bethlehem is a talented harp player. Not only that—he is a brave warrior, a man of war, and has good judgment. He is also a fine-looking young man, and the LORD is with him."

So Saul sent messengers to Jesse to say, "Send me your son David, the shepherd." So David went to Saul and began serving him. Saul loved David very much, and David became his armor bearer. And whenever the tormenting spirit from God troubled Saul, David would play the harp. Then Saul would feel better, and the tormenting spirit would go away. (1 Samuel 16:14-19, 21, 23).

At this point, we see the rise of David, the young shepherd boy

Anointed by God to be the next king of Israel

We also see the beginning of the decline of Saul

And how Saul's wounds surfaces in him

And would lead straight to his own demise

Both physically as well as spiritually

Saul became very angry because of the women's praise of David

His anger would turn to obsessive hate and jealousy for David

The perceived wound in this case is that Saul feels as if he is being overlooked

Disrespected

"Dissed" as the kids would say

With Saul

We see clearly the interplay between our perceived wounds and our actual wounds

The perceived wound was the diss

The actual wounds that arose within Saul

That would later turn into a scar

Are the extreme anger and jealousy

Two evil twins

Sins

> Whatever Saul asked David to do, David did it successfully. So Saul made him a commander over the men of war, an appointment that was welcomed by the people and Saul's officers alike. When the victorious Israelite army was returning home after David had killed the Philistine, women from all the towns of Israel came out to meet King Saul. They sang and danced for joy with tambourines and cymbals. This was their song: "Saul has killed his thousands, and David his ten thousands!" This made Saul very angry. "What's this?" he said. "They credit David with ten thousands and me with only thousands. Next they'll be making him their king!" So from that time on Saul kept a jealous eye on David.

The "tormenting spirit from God" is an evil spirit that God allows to attack

"overwhelmed" Saul
As we have been saying now
Repeatedly
The devil
Satan
Demons
Demon-possessions
Temptations
Are all a part of this life
The battle
God, however, transcends life
God is in control
He may allow even an evil spirit
A demon to accomplish His aim
His goal
As he did in the case of Job
Again
God knows us
God will never put on us more than we can bear
However
God may use our hardened hearts
Our stubbornness
Our lack of faith
To come to the surface
Revel themselves

In order for Him to accomplish His purpose and reveal His power and glory even further

Two things we see happening with Saul
As with Pharaoh
Saul failures
His failure to respect and honor God and His Word
The second thing we see is God using Saul's human failure to exalt His servant David
Again
At any point, Saul could have repented
Change his evil ways
Saul chose not to do so
So it was Saul who rejected God first
God then moved on with His plan and rejected Saul as king

Saul's wounds
The bitter hatred and jealousy toward David
Would grow
And morph into a scar
An even deeper
Dangerous
And threatening wound
This wound
On the part of Saul
Would become a fixation and an obsession

This is the nature of the scar

A wound that won't heal

A wound that won't heal precisely because we refuse to allow it to heal

It is the power we use for evil and not good

It is a power that comes from the devil, not God

In short

Saul became obsessed

He was crumbling

Beginning to lose control

He had

With the help of the enemy

The evil spirit

Ventured out onto that slippery slope of life

The slippery slope that

If we are not careful

We can lose all control

> The very next day a tormenting spirit from God overwhelmed Saul, and he began to rave in his house like a madman. David was playing the harp, as he did each day. But Saul had a spear in his hand, and he suddenly hurled it at David, Intending to pin him to the wall. But David escaped him twice. Saul was then afraid of David, for the LORD was with David and had turned away from Saul (1 Samuel 18:5-12).
>
> David continued to succeed in everything he did, for the LORD was with him. When Saul recognized this, he became even more afraid of him. But all Israel and

> Judah loved David because he was so successful at leading his troops into battle.

Our wounds and our scars can take over our lives

Consume us

Drive us

Direct our every thought and motive

Leading to irrational feelings of fear and loathing

> In the meantime, Saul's daughter Michal had fallen in love with David, and Saul was delighted when he heard about it. "Here's another chance to see him killed by the Philistines!" Saul said to himself. But to David he said, "Today you have a second chance to become my son-in-law!" (1 Samuel 18:14-16, 20-21).
>
> When Saul realized that the LORD was with David and how much his daughter Michal loved him, Saul became even more afraid of him, and he remained David's enemy for the rest of his life (1 Samuel 18:14-16, 20-21).

Saul's Battles Produce His Wounds

Life is a battle

The battle that is life produces, manufactures, and spawns other battles

Saul's battles had become obvious

A feeling of self-doubt

Inadequacy

Lack of confidence

Fear

Lack of faith

Lack of faith in God

Battles produced wounds

The wounds that afflicted Saul were, for the main part, anger and jealousy

The two—anger and jealousy—usually go together

Saul became very angry at what the women were saying

This anger led to extreme jealousy

Saul became jealous of David

As we have been saying, if we are not careful, our wounds can easily turn into scars

This was true of Cain

As we will see, it became true of Saul

Also, we will see that it was true of David

And it can be true in the case of any of us!

Wounds tend to turn into scars

A dangerous wound

A locked-in attitude

An evil, sinful resolve

The scripture says:

> When Saul realized that the LORD was with David and how much his daughter Michal loved him, Saul became even more afraid of him, and he remained

David's enemy for the rest of his life (1 Samuel 18:28-29)

It is important to note that anger and jealousy are sins
A wound is a sin
The devil is not responsible for our sins
God does not cause us to sin
Once again, as the Bible states:

> And remember, when you are being tempted, do not say, "God is tempting me." God is never tempted to do wrong, and he never tempts anyone else. Temptation comes from our own desires, which entice us and drag us away. These desires give birth to sinful actions. And when sin is allowed to grow, it gives birth to death (James 1:13-15).

Wounds turn into wounds that won't heal
Scars
The wounds, anger, and jealousy, almost like twin evils, originated in the heart and mind of Saul

As we have been saying
A wound—real or imagined—can easily and quickly turn into a scar
A heightened, intensified, hardened, crystalized wound that just sets in, that grips you
That won't leave
Again, the scar is a wound
It is a wound that can progress quickly or slowly

It is a wound that we allow to set in

It is a wound that sits and festers

It is a wound that won't heal

It is a wound that we allow to not heal

Wounds that sting

They hurt and cause us pain

They may cause us to overreact

Lash out

It says in 1 Samuel that:

> As Samuel turned to go, Saul tried to hold him back and tore the hem of his robe" (15:27).

Generally, what we perceive as wounds are words and actions done to us that we feel are wrong, that bear the stain of injustice

They cry out for our own form of justice

Some form of revenge

Saul's Wounds Turn into Scars

> When Saul realized that the LORD was with David and how much his daughter Michal loved him, Saul became even more afraid of him, and he remained David's enemy for the rest of his life (1 Samuel 18:28).

This was the moment when Saul's wound turned into a permanent scar!

That would lock in

Become his compulsion

His obsession

That would serve as a point from which it was hard to return

Saul, now, was controlled by his evil emotions and desire

Saul was now about to enter onto that slippery slope

That slippery slope of life where we lose even further control

Remember what we have been saying about entering onto that slippery slope of life?

That sense of losing control

And spiraling out of control

This became the life of King Saul!

> Saul now urged his servants and his son Jonathan to assassinate David. But Jonathan, because of his strong affection for David, told him what his father was planning.
>
> The next morning Jonathan spoke with his father about David, saying many good things about him. "The king must not sin against his servant David," Jonathan said. "He's never done anything to harm you. He has always helped you in any way he could. Have you forgotten about the time he risked his life to kill the Philistine giant and how the LORD brought a great victory to all Israel as a result? You were certainly happy about it then. Why should you murder an innocent man like David? There is no reason for it at all!"
>
> So Saul listened to Jonathan and vowed, "As surely as the LORD lives, David will not be killed." (1 Samuel 19:1-6).

****

But one day when Saul was sitting at home, with spear in hand, the tormenting spirit from the LORD suddenly came upon him again. As David played his harp, Saul hurled his spear at David. But David dodged out of the way, and leaving the spear stuck in the wall, he fled and escaped into the night.

Our wounds

Once they turn into scars

A determined action

Resolve

Becomes like the master

And we the slave

Driven by

Anger

Hatred

Jealousy

And an irrational fear

Then Saul sent troops to watch David's house. They were told to kill David when he came out the next morning. But Michal, David's wife, warned him, "If you don't escape tonight, you will be dead by morning." So she helped him climb out through a window, and he fled and escaped. Then she took an idol and put it in his bed, covered it with blankets, and put a cushion of goat's hair at its head.

The battle is real

Life happens to us

The enemy seeks to invade us

Control us

But God is in control

God is ultimately in control of the battle—and the battles

Satan

By virtue of his usurping the dominion mandate power God gave to the first humans

Has bought for himself a little bit of time before God utterly defeats him and returns the Kingdom of God on Earth back to His most cherished creation

So God is still in control

This is why every time Jesus would come face-to-face with a demon

The demon would protest and say things like this

"Oh no"

"We know who you are, Son of God"

"Have you come to torment us before the time?"

Suggesting that the demons knew their future!

> When the troops came to arrest David, she told them he was sick and couldn't get out of bed. But Saul sent the troops back to get David. He ordered, "Bring him to me in his bed so I can kill him!" But when they came to carry David out, they discovered that it was only an idol in the bed with a cushion of goat's hair at its head (1 Samuel 19:9-16).

> So David escaped and went to Ramah to see Samuel, and he told him all that Saul had done to him. Then Samuel took David with him to live at Naioth. When the report reached Saul that David was at Naioth in Ramah, he sent troops to capture him (1 Samuel 19:18-20).

Our wounds and our scars can be beguiling

Deceiving

Even as we suffer the wounds, we may pretend that everything is all right

We go about our normal functions

Pretending to be normal

> David now fled from Naioth in Ramah and found Jonathan. "What have I done?" he exclaimed. "What is my crime? How have I offended your father that he is so determined to kill me?"
>
> "That's not true!" Jonathan protested. "You're not going to die. He always tells me everything he's going to do, even the little things. I know my father wouldn't hide something like this from me It just isn't so!"
>
> Then David took an oath before Jonathan and said, "Your father knows perfectly well about our friendship, so he has said to himself, 'I won't tell Jonathan—why should I hurt him?' But I swear to you that I am only a step away from death! I swear it by the LORD and by your own soul!"
>
> "Tell me what I can do to help you," Jonathan exclaimed.

David replied, "Tomorrow we celebrate the new moon festival. I've always eaten with the king on this occasion, but tomorrow I'll hide in the field and stay there until the evening of the third day. If your father asks where I am, tell him I asked permission to go home to Bethlehem for an annual family sacrifice (1 Samuel 20:1-6).

So David hid himself in the field, and when the new moon festival began, the king sat down to eat. He sat at his usual place against the wall, with Jonathan sitting opposite him and Abner beside him. But David's place was empty. Saul didn't say anything about it that day, for he said to himself, "Something must have made David ceremonially unclean." But when David's place was empty again the next day, Saul asked Jonathan, "Why hasn't the son of Jesse been here for the meal either yesterday or today?"

We may try to mask our wounds

Our scars

However

They lurk just below the surface, always

They may be unknown to humans

But God sees all

And He gives to servants a discerning spirit

Another thing about these dangerous wounds that we call scars

They may affect our relationships with our friends and family

Jonathan replied, "David earnestly asked me if he could go to Bethlehem. He said, 'Please let me go, for we are having a family sacrifice. My brother demanded that I be there. So please let me get away to see my brothers.' That's why he isn't here at the king's table."

Saul boiled with rage at Jonathan. "You stupid son of a whore!" he swore at him. "Do you think I don't know that you want him to be king in your place, shaming yourself and your mother? As long as that son of Jesse is alive, you'll never be king. Now go and get him so I can kill him!"

"But why should he be put to death?" Jonathan asked his father. "What has he done?"

Then Saul hurled his spear at Jonathan, intending to kill him. So at last Jonathan realized that his father was really determined to kill David.

Jonathan left the table in fierce anger and refused to eat on that second day of the festival, for he was crushed by his father's shameful behavior toward David (1 Samuel 20:24-34, emphasis mine).

Wounds and Scars Create Much Damage

Our wounds, especially when they turn into scars, can affect our relationships

Our relationships with our family

Members of our church family

Our friends

Associates

And the people we work with

How can someone do something so dastardly, we say

We see the images and the stories on TV and in the news

Images and stories where it seems like someone or some group just went berserk

On a rampage

Mowing people down

Usually ending up in their own death as well

"What just happened?" we ask

What is happening to our society and our world?

And we ask questions about the mental and ignore, for the most part, the spiritual

We stray from the Word of God, and God will let us handle our own battles

The best way we can

Make a mess out of our own battles

Without God, we are hopeless in battles

The enemy will eat us alive

And this is what I believe is happening to so many people throughout our world today

Just to touch on this point, human beings are like powerful machines

We can accomplish great and mighty things

However, much like the machine—a bulldozer or tractor—we need a regulator

We need "someone" at the helm or the controls of our lives
Without this regulator, we are out of control
Off the rails
We run amuck
In our thought lives
In our lives
In our decision-making processes
In our thinking
In our decisions
And in our actions
We start relying on our own wisdom

We need to come to our senses and realize that we need God
He, in the form of His Holy Spirit, is our regulator
We need God in all His glory and manifestations
The God we serve is one
The Spirit comes to live on the inside of us
Christ lives
He sits at the right hand of God and intervenes on our behalf
We must think about what we are witnessing in this earthly realm
Really think about it
We can seem like "normal" people

And, at the points of tragedies, we even say this about people

He or she seemed like a fine person!

They were great neighbors—

Until tragedy struck!

These are people who were created by God, in His image, to do great and mighty works

Like the machine

The only thing is that the human machine that runs amuck is bereft of any regulator or regulation

So the machine is out of control

A force other than the "true regulator"

Kind of like a six-year-old

Has gotten behind the controls of the machine

A machine that was created to do good works turns into a destructive, deadly, killing machine, destroying everything in its path, even him or herself

On the one hand, it reflects the power of the machine

On the other hand, it reflects what this machine, this powerful human being, is capable of without the presence of the regulator, or Spirit of God

Or it shows, on the other hand, what the human/machine can do in the hands of another regulator

This is too many of us

Human beings without God in our lives

Then we stand in shock and awe

How can someone just decapitate another human being?

How can someone just take a gun or a weapon and mow down countless people?

We are confused

We are left scratching our heads

Sometimes, we say

Oh, he or she was my neighbor

They seemed like such wonderful people

The truth is life is a battle

Battles produce wounds

What we are seeing plenty of in our world is the "work" of the "wounded" among us

Again, keep in mind wounds don't have to be real

They can be real or imagined

We may not believe in an enemy of God and mankind

However, he exists

And he is prepared to take full advantage of our "feelings" of having been wounded

He helps turn the wounds into scars by turning us away from Truth

Not the truth

But Truth!

The scars are the wounds that become entrenched

The wounds that won't heal

The wounds that we do not allow to heal

The scars take us deeper and deeper into sin

They carry us out onto the slippery slope of life, where it is hard to return from

The scars can cause us to lose control

Spiral out of control

Spiral completely out of control

Leading to much death and destruction

Even our own death and destruction!

> So David escaped from Saul and went to King Achish of Gath. Then Doeg the Edomite, who was standing there with Saul's men, spoke up.
>
> "When I was at Nob," he said, "I saw the son of Jesse talking to the priest, Ahimelech son of Ahitub. Ahimelech consulted the LORD for him. Then he gave him food and the sword of Goliath the Philistine" (1 Samuel 21:10, 22:9-10).
>
> King Saul immediately sent for Ahimelech and all his family, who served as priests at Nob. When they arrived, Saul shouted at him, "Listen to me, you son of Ahitub!"
>
> "What is it, my king?" Ahimelech asked.
>
> "Why have you and the son of Jesse conspired against me?" Saul demanded. "Why did you give him food and a sword? Why have you consulted God for him? Why have you encouraged him to kill me, as he is trying to do this very day?"
>
> "But sir," Ahimelech replied. "Is anyone among all your servants as faithful as David, your son-in-law? Why, he is the captain of your bodyguard and a

highly honored member of your household! This was certainly not the first time I had consulted God for him! May the king not accuse me and my family in this matter, for I knew nothing at all of any plot against you."

"You will surely die, Ahimelech, along with your entire family!" the king shouted. And he ordered his bodyguards, "Kill these priests of the Lord, for they are allies and conspirators with David! They knew he was running away from me, but they didn't tell me!" But Saul's men refused to kill the Lord's priests.

Then the king said to Doeg, "You do it." So Doeg the Edomite turned on them and killed them that day, eighty-five priests in all, still wearing their priestly garments. Then he went to Nob, the town of the priests, and killed the priests' families—men and women, children and babies—and all the cattle, donkeys, sheep, and goats. Only Abiathar, one of the sons of Ahimelech, escaped and fled to David (1 Samuel 22:11-20).

Our Scars can cause us to spiral out of control

Our wounds, when they turn into scars, can cause us to lose control

To spiral out of control

To spiral completely out of control

The Philistines set up their camp at Shunem, and Saul gathered all the army of Israel and camped at Gilboa. When Saul saw the vast Philistine army, he became frantic with fear. He asked the LORD what he should do, but the LORD refused to answer him, either by dreams or by sacred lots or by the prophets. Saul then said to his advisers, "Find a woman who is a medium, so I can go and ask her what to do." His advisers replied, "There is a medium at Endor."

So Saul disguised himself by wearing ordinary clothing instead of his royal robes. Then he went to the woman's home at night, accompanied by two of his men. "I have to talk to a man who has died," he said. "Will you call up his spirit for me?"

"Are you trying to get me killed?" the woman demanded. "You know that Saul has outlawed all the mediums and all who consult the spirits of the dead. Why are you setting a trap for me?"

But Saul took an oath in the name of the LORD and promised, "As surely as the LORD lives, nothing bad will happen to you for doing this."

Finally, the woman said, "Well, whose spirit do you want me to call up?" "Call up Samuel," Saul replied.

When the woman saw Samuel, she screamed, "You've deceived me! You are Saul!"

"Don't be afraid!" the king told her. "What do you see?"

"I see a god coming up out of the earth," she said.

"What does he look like?" Saul asked.

"He is an old man wrapped in a robe," she replied. Saul realized it was Samuel, and he fell to the ground before him.

"Why have you disturbed me by calling me back?" Samuel asked Saul.

"Because I am in deep trouble," Saul replied. "The Philistines are at war with me, and God has left me and won't reply by prophets or dreams. So I have called for you to tell me what to do."

But Samuel replied, "Why ask me, since the LORD has left you and has become your enemy? The LORD has done just as he said he would. He has torn the kingdom from you and given it to your rival, David. The LORD has done this to you today because you refused to carry out his fierce anger against the Amalekites. What's more, the LORD will hand you and the army of Israel over to the Philistines tomorrow, and you and your sons will be here with me. The LORD will bring down the entire army of Israel in defeat."

Saul fell full length on the ground, paralyzed with fright because of Samuel's words. He was also faint with hunger, for he had eaten nothing all day and all night.

When the woman saw how distraught he was, she said, "Sir, I obeyed your command at the risk of my life. Now do what I say, and let me give you a little something to eat so you can regain your strength for the trip back" But Saul refused to eat anything. Then his advisers joined the woman in urging him to eat. So he finally yielded and got up from the ground and sat on the couch. The woman had been fattening a calf, so she hurried out and killed it. She took some flour, kneaded it into dough and baked unleavened bread. She brought the meal to Saul and his advisers, and they ate it. Then they went out into the night (1 Samuel 28:4-25).

This series of events marked the turning point in Saul's life
How the wounds of anger and jealousy crippled his life
Destroyed his life physically and spiritually
Saul's life clearly showed how our wounds can turn into scars
How the scars can cause us to lose control

Spiral out of control
This is the unraveling of the king
A pitiable sight
A life spiraling completely out of control
A point of no return!
All because of Saul's wound that would not heal
All because of a wound that turned into a scar

> Now the Philistines attacked Israel, and the men of Israel fled before them. Many were slaughtered on the slopes of Mount Gilboa. The Philistines closed in on Saul and his sons, and they killed three of his sons—Jonathan, Abinadab, and Malkishua. The fighting grew very fierce around Saul, and the Philistine archers caught up with him and wounded him severely. Saul groaned to his armor bearer, "Take your sword and kill me before these pagan Philistines come to run me through and taunt and torture me." But his armor bearer was afraid and would not do it. So Saul took his own sword and fell on it. When his armor bearer realized that Saul was dead, he fell on his own sword and died beside the king. So Saul, his three sons, his armor bearer, and his troops all died together that same day (1 Samuel 31:1-6).

Indeed, the scars are deadly!
They can doom us
Rob of us life
They can lead to our spiritual and physical death!
Most important, they can rob us of our God-given potential and purpose

By the way, this is the goal of the enemy
The devil
To rob this world
This life
To rob God
Of every human soul and purpose that is precious to God

Of course
We
Generally speaking
We don't want to believe in the spirit world
In demons
This, too, is a sign of a lack of faith
We want to bundle up all phenomena and crowd it into the category of mental health
Mental illness
Much to our own detriment
However
The Bible teaches that the spirit world is real
Demons are real
Satan
The devil
Once known as Lucifer
Is real
and they are all a part of the lives of us humans
a part of the battle—and the battles—we face

CHAPTER 10

David's Journey through the battle and the battles without the Scars—Almost!

No one is above falling victim to the wounds and the scars of life

We might think we are

The Bible says:

If you think you are standing strong, be careful you don't fall

> If you think you are standing strong, be careful not to fall (1 Corinthians 10:12).

We are all in a battle

We are all susceptible to the battles of life

God chose David to be the second king of Israel

David replaced Saul

David was a warrior king

He fought in and led numerous battles

God blessed David

Under David, the kingdom of Israel was united

Flourished

It abounded in peace, prosperity, and wealth

Our Biggest Enemy in Battle

Think about David

God called him a man after His own heart!

As the prophet Nathan said about David, he had it all!

What makes powerful men and women fall?

Kings and queens

Presidents of the world's most powerful countries

Even as they are riding a wave of success and popularity in the polls

Among public opinion

What is that fatal weapon that causes it to all come crumbling and crashing down

What is the weapon?

The enemy?

It's not the enemy that we know and we commonly think of as the enemy

No

The enemy

The greatest enemy of humans is not people

Satan

Evil spirits or demons

The greatest enemy to humans is self!

That very human part of us, known as "the flesh"

The residence of our human emotions and desires that gives rise to our wounds

The wounds that oftentimes turn into scars!

We battle

We cave

In and of ourselves, we cannot win

We give in to our very evil

Sinful human emotions and desires

That all-too-human part of ourselves

That part the Bible calls "the flesh"

The seat and base of our emotions and desires

The Importance of Living a Productive and Purposeful Life

Living a productive and purposeful life is one of the keys to going through the battles without incurring the scars

The key to understanding our purpose in life and leading a productive life is, of course, a relationship with God

God wants us to be productive

Being productive in life can keep us out of "trouble"
The Bible says:

> In the spring of the year, when kings normally go out to war, David sent Joab and the Israelite army to fight the Ammonites. They destroyed the Ammonite army and laid siege to the city of Rabbah. However, David stayed behind in Jerusalem (2 Samuel 11:1).

The Beginning of David's Wound

David's wound was greed

Covetousness

It led him to commit adultery with Bathsheba

David's wound would turn into a scar

He became committed to going down a wrong path

A path that, deep down inside, David must have known was wrong

> Late one afternoon, after his midday rest, David got out of bed and was walking on the roof of the palace. As he looked out over the city, he noticed a woman of unusual beauty taking a bath. He sent someone to find out who she was, and he was told, "She is Bathsheba, the daughter of Eliam and the wife of Uriah the Hittite." Then David sent messengers to get her, and when she came to the palace, he slept with her (2 Samuel 11:2-4).

Let us not ever underestimate the power of our wounds

The scars

A bit of advice for men—and women

Men, take my advice

Women, you do likewise

When we see an "unusually" attractive woman or man

One who is not our wife or husband

We should run

Not just run

But run fast!

Real fast!

Don't even stop to take a second look

Sometimes, I think it is that second look that gets us (just kidding—though I am not!)

Do like Joseph and run

Leave your cloak behind if you have to

When I was in college, during one of my many lapses in judgment

Just being young, carefree

I started hanging out with some students and non-students who were engaged in political activities on the university campus

They called themselves "activists" and "revolutionaries"

In hindsight, they nor I had any real concept of what it means to be "a revolutionary"

It just sounded cool

The in thing

"hip!"

Especially if you were a minority and felt like you were being "oppressed"

These friends of mine convinced me to join their political activism

They convinced me to take classes outside of my major

Classes like Marxist-Socialist Economic Theory and Introduction to Logic

Somehow, they had convinced me that if I wanted to be a true revolutionary, these were some of the classes I *had* to take

Like a dummy, I just went along

I was a smart student

In my area of specialization, that is!

Both of these classes had my head spinning

They were clearly out of my league

Especially Introduction to Logic

The professor, a real affable gentleman—seeing that I had absolutely no chance of passing the class—decided to "set me up" with a tutor

I called her up

Agreed to meet her at her apartment the next Friday night

This was my first mistake

When I went over and gently knocked on the door

And the door opened

I stumbled back

Gulped

In the doorway was a slender, very attractive young woman

However, what made matters even worse

And sent me in fast retreat from that door

Was the fact that she was clad only in a white, loosely buttoned down, short—even by her standard—men's Oxford shirt

My internal battle did not last very long

I was scared for my life!

In spite of a quickly onsetting wound

I managed to beat a hasty retreat away from that door that night

Thank God!

I just remember hearing myself say

Never mind!

That's okay

But thank you very much!

And

I have to go!

I think I have been leery—and cautious—of any "unusually" attractive woman ever since

What causes one to sin

And creates in us a wound

That can lead to a dangerous and deadly scar

Yes, what causes us to sin can be most attractive!

David's actions and behaviors after his crime clearly showed that he knew that what he had done was wrong

> Then David sent word to Joab: "Send me Uriah the Hittite." So Joab sent him to David. When Uriah arrived, David asked him how Joab and the army were getting along and how the war was progressing. Then he told Uriah, "Go on home and relax. David even sent a gift to Uriah after he had left the palace. But Uriah didn't go home. He slept that night at the palace entrance with the king's palace guard (2 Samuel 11:6-9).

****

> So the next morning David wrote a letter to Joab and gave it to Uriah to deliver. The letter instructed Joab, "Station Uriah on the front lines where the battle is fiercest. Then pull back so that he will be killed" (2 Samuel 11:14-15).

This reminds me of an old song that says

Sin will take you farther than you want to go, and keep you there longer than you want to stay

Remember, our reaction to a wound can be a sin

A wound, once it becomes a scar, is a sin

A unique type of sin

In that God has given us control over how we react to our wounds

Not to excuse David in any way, but what the story of David and Bathsheba shows us is that life is a battle

No one

No matter how great or small

Rich or poor

King or pauper

No one is exempt from battles

Battles, as we have been saying, produce wounds

The battle, for David, had to do with whether or not to go after Bathsheba

To have her brought over to the palace or not

Resisting or not resisting the urge to do so

Lust

Greed

David's battle, like ours, also involved choosing to go God's way or his own

Again, David's wound was lust

The scar was once David was determined

Locked into his decision

Another thing that the story shows us is how our response to the wounds we experience in battles can have far-reaching consequences

Far-reaching consequences in both this life and the next

Life is a battle

As a battle, life produces, manufactures, and spawns other battles

Battles produce wounds
Wounds can and do turn into scars
A scar can develop suddenly
In an instant
Or over time
It did not take long for David's wound to turn into a scar
It says:

> [David] sent someone to find out who she was, and he was told, "She is Bathsheba, the daughter of Eliam and the wife of Uriah the Hittite." Then David sent messengers to get her (2 Samuel 11:3-4, parenthesis mine).

David's sin, his mortal wound, also shows how we live our lives at the intersection of our battles and our wounds
Mortal because David's sin cost him his life
David was good as dead
We can say that God brought David back to life
He forgave him

When we are wounded, it becomes a pivotal moment in and of our lives
A crossroad
A moment of decision
Just as it was in the case of Cain, it was here at this life-changing intersection where David had to choose
Like Cain, David could choose life

Or he could choose death

David, like Cain, could choose to do "the right thing," which was to follow God's Word, or the wrong thing, reject the Word of God

Finally, like Cain—and Saul—David chose death

The wages of sin is death

From that moment, David became a dead man walking

David was, at this moment, a condemned rebel!

Death became his fate

As a matter of fact, his own words condemned him

Only the grace of God saved David

The words of the prophet, Nathan, bear this out:

> So the LORD sent Nathan the prophet to tell David this story: "There were two men in a certain town. One was rich, and one was poor. The rich man owned a great many sheep and cattle. The poor man owned nothing but one little lamb he had bought. He raised that little lamb, and it grew up with his children. It ate from the man's own plate and drank from his cup. He cuddled it in his arms like a baby daughter. One day a guest arrived at the home of the rich man. But instead of killing an animal from his own flock or herd, he took the poor man's lamb and killed it and prepared it for his guest."
>
> David was furious. "As surely as the LORD lives," he vowed, "any man who would do such a thing deserves to die! He must repay four lambs to the poor man for the one he stole and for having no pity."
>
> Then Nathan said to David, "You are that man! The LORD, the God of Israel, says: I anointed you king

of Israel and saved you from the power of Saul. I gave you your master's house and his wives and the kingdoms of Israel and Judah. And if that had not been enough, I would have given you much, much more. Why, then, have you despised the word of the LORD and done this horrible deed? For you have murdered Uriah the Hittite with the sword of the Ammonites and stolen his wife. From this time on, your family will live by the sword because you have despised me by taking Uriah's wife to be your own. "This is what the LORD says: Because of what you have done, I will cause your own household to rebel against you. I will give your wives to another man before your very eyes, and he will go to bed with them in public view. You did it secretly, but I will make this happen to you openly in the sight of all Israel" (2 Samuel 12:1-12).

Then David confessed to Nathan, "I have sinned against the LORD."

Nathan replied, "Yes, but the LORD has forgiven you, and you won't die for this sin. Nevertheless, because you have shown utter contempt for the word of the LORD by doing this, your child will die" (2 Samuel 12:13-14).

Our wounds, when they turn into scars, can be most agonizing

We actually give up our freedom

The right to be free

We find ourselves at the mercy of a righteous and merciful God

Wounds, we said, hurt

They are painful

In other words, they cause us pain

They introduce into our lives a painful and tortuous reality of vulnerability

We lose control

At this point in the progression of our wound, there is absolutely nothing we can do

> After Nathan returned to his home, the LORD sent a deadly illness to the child of David and Uriah's wife. David begged God to spare the child. He went without food and lay all night on the bare ground. The elders of his household pleaded with him to get up and eat with them, but he refused. Then on the seventh day the child died. David's advisers were afraid to tell him.
>
> "He wouldn't listen to reason while the child was ill" they said. "What drastic thing will he do when we tell him the child is dead?"
>
> When David saw them whispering, he realized what had happened. "Is the child dead?" he asked.
>
> "Yes," they replied, "he is dead."
>
> Then David got up from the ground, washed himself, put on lotions, and changed his clothes. He went to the Tabernacle and worshiped the LORD. After that, he returned to the palace and was served food and ate.
>
> His advisers were amazed. "We don't understand you," they told him. "While the child was still living, you wept and refused to eat. But now that the child is dead, you have stopped your mourning and are eating again."

> David replied, "I fasted and wept while the child was alive, for I said, 'Perhaps the LORD will be gracious to me and let the child live.' But why should I fast when he is dead? Can I bring him back again? I will go to him one day, but he cannot return to me" (2 Samuel 12:15-23).

The wages of sin
The consequence of sin
Is death

The scars can lead to much death and destruction
This was the case for David's family for many years
As the prophet, Nathan, pronounced

> From this time on, your family will live by the sword because you have despised me by taking Uriah's wife to be your own. "This is what the LORD says: Because of what you have done, I will cause your own household to rebel against you. I will give your wives to another man before your very eyes, and he will go to bed with them in public view. You did it secretly, but I will make this happen to you openly in the sight of all Israel" (2 Samuel 12:10-12).

So, there is always a response on our part to our wounds
No matter how painful
No matter difficult
We choose how to respond
Once we have made a conscious decision, we lock in this decision

Then we act

Two things are central to our decision-making

Our choosing

Or our choices

What we want

Or what the Word of God says

This is why a relationship with God and His Word is so vital

We need help making right decisions

This help can reside on the inside of us

The Bible says:

> Trust in the LORD with all your heart; do not depend on your own understanding. Seek his will in all you do, and he will show you which path to take (Proverbs 3:5-6).

David lost his battle

His wound of greed

Covetousness

Lust

Quickly turned into a scar

A wound that would not heal

A wound that David did not allow to heal

A wound that became the source of much grief, sorrow, and death in the life of David and his immediate family

When David's Wound Almost Cost Him His Life

Our scars are dangerous

They are deadly

They can upend our lives

Most importantly, they can rob us of our God-given potential and purpose

The Bible says:

> Then David moved down to the wilderness of Maon. There was a wealthy man from Maon who owned property near the town of Carmel. He had 3,000 sheep and 1,000 goats, and it was sheep-shearing time. This man's name was Nabal, and his wife, Abigail, was a sensible and beautiful woman. But Nabal, a descendant of Caleb, was crude and mean in all his dealings.
>
> When David heard that Nabal was shearing his sheep, he sent ten of his young men to Carmel with this message for Nabal: "Peace and prosperity to you, your family, and everything you own! I am told that it is sheep-shearing time. While your shepherds stayed among us near Carmel, we never harmed them, and nothing was ever stolen from them. Ask your own men, and they will tell you this is true. So would you be kind to us, since we have come at a time of celebration? Please share any provisions you might have on hand with us and with your friend David." David's young men gave this message to Nabal in David's name, and they waited for a reply.
>
> "Who is this fellow David?" Nabal sneered to the young men. "Who does this son of Jesse think he is? There are lots of servants these days who run away from their masters. Should I take my bread and my

water and my meat that I've slaughtered for my shearers and give it to a band of outlaws who come from who knows where?"

So David's young men returned and told him what Nabal had said. "Get your swords!" was David's reply as he strapped on his own. (1 Samuel 25:1-13).

Pause!

Freeze!

Right here

In an instant, David's wound turned into a scar

A scar can develop instantly or over time

David was wounded

Nabal had insulted him

Belittled him

Wronged him

Especially since, in David's view, he and his men had provided protection for Nabal's shepherds near Carmel

David had already determined

Locked in

In his mind, he already knew what he would do

No

What needed to be done!

In other words, the wound had already turned into a scar!

Then 400 men started off with David, and 200 remained behind to guard their equipment

The Bible says that God
In his infinite love and mercy
Declared that it was not good for the man to be alone
So God decided in His great wisdom
To create
The Bible says
"A helper who is just right for Him!"[2]
(Lord, help me, here—I am going to get myself in trouble!)
This is a very powerful statement!
This statement doesn't just apply to Adam and Eve
The first humans
I submit to you that this statement is a principle that can and must be applied to the lives of all women and men everywhere!
A woman was conceived in the mind of the Creator
She was designed
And created
To be a helper
A helper for the man
The male!
To complement him!
This does not make her less than a man
Or inferior to man
In fact, she is his equal

---

[2] Genesis 2:18

But her purpose in life is to come alongside to help the male

Helping

Supporting

Comes natural to a woman

A female

Much more so than to a man

A man

Generally speaking is more selfish—if you know what I mean!

Oftentimes, this helpful nature may translate into helping him succeed

Helping to save his life

But whatever it is, she serves this invaluable role and purpose in life of helping her male counterpart

A woman is oftentimes smarter than a man

More discerning

Better at planning

And executing!

A woman may just let her man *think* that he is better at certain things

She is propping him up!

Notice?

Helping him!

This was Abigail

The beautiful and intelligent wife of foolish Nabal, a wealthy but crude rancher and businessman

> Meanwhile, one of Nabal's servants went to Abigail and told her, "David sent messengers from the wilderness to greet our master. But he screamed insults at them. These men have been very good to us, and we never suffered any harm from them. Nothing was stolen from us the whole time they were with us. In fact, day and night they were like a wall of protection to us and the sheep. You need to know this and figure out what to do, for there is going to be trouble for our master and his whole family. He's so ill-tempered that no one can even talk to him!"

I want you to watch this brave

Quick thinking

Smart

Intelligent woman spring into action

With God's help, and by His grace

She is going to help save the lives of

Not just one

But two men this day!

> Abigail wasted no time. She quickly gathered 200 loaves of bread, two wineskins full of wine, five sheep that had been slaughtered, nearly a bushel of roasted grain, 100 clusters of raisins, and 200 fig cakes. She packed them on donkeys and said to her servants, "Go on ahead. I will follow you shortly." But she didn't tell her husband Nabal what she was doing.

Please note that David has been "wounded'

"Disrespected" by

In his mind

An ungrateful

Foolish Nabal

And David is partly right

Nabal should have known better than to pick a fight with David—the mightiest warrior in the land

Also, notice how this perceived wound on the part of David would turn into a real wound

A wound that would imperil his life

Destroy his whole potential and purpose in life

Abigail tells him so much when she hurries out to meet him

She could "smell" a battle brewing

And she knew

Just "knew" nothing good was going to come out of this conflict

This war

The power of a woman!

> As she was riding her donkey into a mountain ravine, she saw David and his men coming toward her. David had just been saying, "A lot of good it did to help this fellow. We protected his flocks in the wilderness, and nothing he owned was lost or stolen. But he has repaid me evil for good. May God strike me and kill me if even one man of his household is still alive tomorrow morning!"
>
> When Abigail saw David, she quickly got off her donkey and bowed low before him. She fell at his feet and said, "I accept all blame in this matter, my lord. Please listen to what I have to say. I know Nabal is a wicked and ill-tempered man; please don't pay

any attention to him. He is a fool, just as his name suggests. But I never even saw the young men you sent. "Now, my lord, as surely as the LORD lives and you yourself live, since the LORD has kept you from murdering and taking vengeance into your own hands, let all your enemies and those who try to harm you be as cursed as Nabal is.

And here is a present that I, your servant, have brought to you and your young men. Please forgive me if I have offended you in any way. The LORD will surely reward you with a lasting dynasty, for you are fighting the LORD's battles. And you have not done wrong throughout your entire life. Even when you are chased by those who seek to kill you, your life is safe in the care of the LORD your God, secure in his treasure pouch! But the lives of your enemies will disappear like stones shot from a sling! When the LORD has done all he promised and has made you leader of Israel, don't let this be a blemish on your record. Then your conscience won't have to bear the staggering burden of needless bloodshed and vengeance. And when the LORD has done these great things for you, please remember me, your servant!"

David proves himself, in this instance, to not be much better than foolish Nabal

But this is what a wound will do to us

Anger

Anger will cause us to lose control

Lose control of our faculties

Lose control of ourselves

And lose control of our lives!

> David replied to Abigail, "Praise the LORD, the God of Israel, who has sent you to meet me today! Thank God for your good sense! Bless you for keeping me from murder and from carrying out vengeance with my own hands (1 Samuel 25:14-33).

It's like our wounds—anger, in this particular case—can cause us to suffer from temporary insanity!

Cause us to forget

Bypass

The Word of God

> For I swear by the LORD, the God of Israel, who has kept me from hurting you, that if you had not hurried out to meet me, not one of Nabal's men would still be alive tomorrow morning." Then David accepted her present and told her, "Return home in peace. I have heard what you said. We will not kill your husband" (1 Samuel 25:34-35).

The Hidden Danger in Our Anger

This story illustrates, among other things, the danger of anger

Not controlling our temper

How quickly our temper can get out of control

Become a heightened wound

Turn into a scar

Nabal's harsh and un-wise

Ill-timed words

Were unfortunate

David perceived them as an insult

Disrespect

Unfair

Unjust

Remember

Wounds can be real or imagined

Even though, based on the testimony of all who knew Nabal, David had good grounds to be upset

The insult turned to anger

And his anger led David to a desire for revenge

Taking matters into his own hands

Without the swift and timely intervention on the part of Abigail, Nabal's wife, and a woman that David would later marry, the wound that David suffered—and the scar that it quickly turned into—would have led to much death and destruction that day

Possibly even robbing David of his divine potential and purpose

This story, perhaps like no other, highlights the dangerous and potentially deadly and destructive nature of the scars

CHAPTER 11

A Man After God's Own Heart

Except for his sin with Bathsheba, David lived a model life of going through the battle—and the battles—without incurring the scars of life

David

As far as the wounds and the scars are concerned, not counting his moral debacle with Bathsheba

Which he paid a devastating price for

David lived a life of freedom

Having a clear conscience

And a life pleasing to God

A life of love

Mercy

Grace

Kindness

And forgiveness

David
Like Joseph
Understood the centrality of God's Word to his life
Not just knowing it
Quoting it
But the importance of living one's life in complete obedience to God and His Word
Trusting it
Relying on it
Standing on it
Doing what it says
Truly loving God

We live in a world where so many of us know the Word
We tout at every turn how well-versed we are in it
We like to quote it
On Facebook and other social media
The question is, though, do we really understand the value and the purpose of God's Word?
Do we allow it to really impact our lives?
Are we standing on the promises of God?
Are we treating God's Word for what it is?
Principles to live on—and by?
Jesus said:

If you hear my words and do them! (Matthew 7:24)

Simply hearing the Word and merely quoting it

But not allowing it to penetrate down deep and steer our lives is nothing new

The scripture says—God says:

These people say they are mine. They honor me with their lips, but their hearts are far from me (Isaiah 29:13).

David said:

> I have hidden your word in my heart, that I might not sin against you (Psalm 119:11).

and

> Your word is a lamp to guide my feet and a light for my path (Psalm 119:105).

David's Acts of Kindness and Forgiveness

David strove to live out his life in accordance with the Word of God

David knew Jesus

Saw Him

Jesus

The manifest Word of God

David said:

> The LORD said to my Lord, "Sit in the place of honor at my right hand until I humble your enemies, making them a footstool under your feet" (Psalm 110:1).

David followed the teachings of Jesus
One of Jesus' main tenants
Loving and forgiving everyone
Including your enemy!

> After Saul returned from fighting the Philistines, he was told that David had gone into the wilderness of En-gedi. So Saul chose 3,000 elite troops from all Israel and went to search for David and his men near the rocks of the wild goats.
>
> At the place where the road passes some sheepfolds, Saul went into a cave to relieve himself. But as it happened, David and his men were hiding farther back in that very cave!
>
> "Now's your opportunity!" David's men whispered to him. "Today the LORD is telling you, 'I will certainly put your enemy into your power, to do with as you wish.'" So David crept forward and cut off a piece of the hem of Saul's robe.

But David instinctively knew the Word of God
Like all of us
It was also written in his heart
His conscience telling him it was not the right thing to do

> But then David's conscience began bothering him because he had cut Saul's robe. He said to his men, "The LORD forbid that I should do this to my lord

the king. I shouldn't attack the LORD's anointed one, for the LORD himself has chosen him." So David restrained his men and did not let them kill Saul.

After Saul had left the cave and gone on his way, David came out and shouted after him, "My lord the king!" And when Saul looked around, David bowed low before him.

Then he shouted to Saul, "Why do you listen to the people who say I am trying to harm you? This very day you can see with your own eyes it isn't true. For the LORD placed you at my mercy back there in the cave. Some of my men told me to kill you, but I spared you. For I said, 'I will never harm the king—he is the LORD's anointed one.' Look, my father, at what I have in my hand. It is a piece of the hem of your robe! I cut it off, but I didn't kill you. This proves that I am not trying to harm you and that I have not sinned against you, even though you have been hunting for me to kill me.

David, here, is standing rock solid on the Word of God
It touches
And informs
His life!

"May the LORD judge between us. Perhaps the LORD will punish you for what you are trying to do to me, but I will never harm you. As that old proverb says, 'From evil people come evil deeds.' So you can be sure I will never harm you. Who is the king of Israel trying to catch anyway? Should he spend his time chasing one who is as worthless as a dead dog or a single flea? May the LORD therefore judge which of us is right and punish the guilty one. He is my advocate, and he will rescue me from your power!"

> When David had finished speaking, Saul called back, "Is that really you, my son David?" Then he began to cry. And he said to David, "You are a better man than I am, for you have repaid me good for evil. Yes, you have been amazingly kind to me today, for when the LORD put me in a place where you could have killed me, you didn't do it. Who else would let his enemy get away when he had him in his power? May the LORD reward you well for the kindness you have shown me today. And now I realize that you are surely going to be king, and that the kingdom of Israel will flourish under your rule (1 Samuel 24:1-20).

David shows mercy to Saul yet again:

> Now some men from Ziph came to Saul at Gibeah to tell him, "David is hiding on the hill of Hakilah, which overlooks Jeshimon." So Saul took 3,000 of Israel's elite troops and went to hunt him down in the wilderness of Ziph. Saul camped along the road beside the hill of Hakilah, near Jeshimon, where David was hiding. When David learned that Saul had come after him into the wilderness he sent out spies to verify the report of Saul's arrival.
>
> David slipped over to Saul's camp one night to look around. Saul and Abner son of Ner, the commander of his army, were sleeping inside a ring formed by the slumbering warriors. "Who will volunteer to go in there with me?" David asked Ahimelech the Hittite and Abishai son of Zeruiah, Joab's brother.
>
> "I'll go with you," Abishai replied. So David and Abishai went right into Saul's camp and found him asleep, with his spear stuck in the ground beside his head. Abner and the soldiers were lying asleep around him.

> "God has surely handed your enemy over to you this time!" Abishai whispered to David. "Let me pin him to the ground with one thrust of the spear. I won't need to strike twice!"
>
> "No!" David said. "Don't kill him. For who can remain innocent after attacking the LORD's anointed one? Surely the LORD will strike Saul down someday, or he will die of old age or in battle. The LORD forbid that I should kill the one he has anointed! But take his spear and that jug of water beside his head, and then let's get out of here!"

We can clearly see why God said about David

David is a man after My own heart

David is a paragon

A model picture of love and forgiveness

Peter once asked Jesus how many times a person should forgive another person

Peter wanted to know if seven times would suffice

But Jesus said no

Seventy times seven

In other words

Infinitely

We get the distinct impression that David had internalize—and prepared to live out—this teaching

> So David took the spear and jug of water that were near Saul's head. Then he and Abishai got away without anyone seeing them or even waking up, because the LORD had put Saul's men into a deep sleep.

David climbed the hill opposite the camp until he was at a safe distance. Then he shouted down to the soldiers and to Abner son of Ner, "Wake up, Abner!"

"Who is it?" Abner demanded.

"Well, Abner, you're a great man, aren't you?" David taunted. "Where in all Israel is there anyone as mighty?

So why haven't you guarded your master the king when someone came to kill him? This isn't good at all! I swear by the LORD that you and your men deserve to die, because you failed to protect your master, the LORD's anointed! Look around! Where are the king's spear and the jug of water that were beside his head?"

Saul recognized David's voice and called out, "Is that you, my son David?"

And David replied, "Yes, my lord the king. Why are you chasing me? What have I done? What is my crime? But now let my lord the king listen to his servant. If the LORD has stirred you up against me, then let him accept my offering. But if this is simply a human scheme, then may those involved be cursed by the LORD. For they have driven me from my home, so I can no longer live among the LORD's people. And they have said, 'Go, worship pagan gods.' Must I die on foreign soil, far from the presence of the LORD? Why has the king of Israel come out to search for a single flea? Why does he hunt me down like a partridge on the mountains?"

Then Saul confessed, "I have sinned. Come back home, my son, and I will no longer try to harm you, for you valued my life today. I have been a fool and very, very wrong."

"Here is your spear, O king," David replied. "Let one of your young men come over and get it. The LORD gives his own reward for doing good and for being loyal, and I refused to kill you even when the LORD placed you in my power, for you are the LORD's anointed one. Now may the LORD value my life, even as I have valued yours today. May he rescue me from all my troubles."

And Saul said to David, "Blessings on you, my son David. You will do many heroic deeds, and you will surely succeed." Then David went away, and Saul returned home (1 Samuel 26:1-25).

David: The Heart of God

David's life
Apart from his sin with Bathsheba
Was a demonstration of grace, love, and tender mercy)
The story of Mephibosheth is perhaps one of the most touching and revealing stories in the Bible
It speaks to how God desires for us to live
It is a story of compassionate love, grace, and mercy
A similar story
One that Jesus told
Is the story of the Good Samaritan

First, the story of Mephibosheth

One day David asked, "Is anyone in Saul's family still alive—anyone to whom I can show kindness for Jonathan's sake?" He summoned a man named Ziba, who had been one of Saul's servants. "Are you Ziba?" the king asked.

"Yes sir, I am," Ziba replied.

The king then asked him, "Is anyone still alive from Saul's family? If so, I want to show God's kindness to them."

Ziba replied, "Yes, one of Jonathan's sons is still alive. He is crippled in both feet."

"Where is he?" the king asked.

"In Lo-debar," Ziba told him, "at the home of Makir son of Ammiel."

So David sent for him and brought him from Makir's home. His name was Mephibosheth; he was Jonathan's son and Saul's grandson. When he came to David, he bowed low to the ground in deep respect. David said, "Greetings, Mephibosheth."

Mephibosheth replied, "I am your servant."

"Don't be afraid!" David said. "I intend to show kindness to you because of my promise to your father, Jonathan. I will give you all the property that once belonged to your grandfather Saul, and you will eat here with me at the king's table!"

Mephibosheth bowed respectfully and exclaimed, "Who is your servant, that you should show such kindness to a dead dog like me?"

Then the king summoned Saul's servant Ziba and said, "I have given your master's grandson everything that belonged to Saul and his family. You and your sons and servants are to farm the land for him to produce food for your master's household. But Mephibosheth, your master's grandson, will eat here at my table." (Ziba had fifteen sons and twenty servants.)

Ziba replied, "Yes, my lord the king; I am your servant, and I will do all that you have commanded." And from that time on, Mephibosheth ate regularly at David's table, like one of the king's own sons (2 Samuel 9:1-11).

****

It is important for us to understand the battle that is life

And the battles produced by—and in life

They all belong to God

We may not know or understand why we are going through a rough spell in our lives

We may not realize that God may be allowing us to go through the battle

The fire

The storm

The difficulty

David alludes to God being in control when he was fleeing from his son Absalom after Absalom rebelled against him

> As King David came to Bahurim, a man came out of the village cursing them. It was Shimei son of Gera, from the same clan as Saul's family. He threw stones at the king and the king's officers and all the mighty warriors who surrounded him. "Get out of here, you murderer, you scoundrel!" he shouted at David. "The LORD is paying you back for all the bloodshed in

Saul's clan. You stole his throne, and now the LORD has given it to your son Absalom. At last you will taste some of your own medicine, for you are a murderer!"

"Why should this dead dog curse my lord the king?" Abishai son of Zeruiah demanded. "Let me go over and cut off his head!"

"No!" the king said. "Who asked your opinion, you sons of Zeruiah! If the LORD has told him to curse me, who are you to stop him?"

Then David said to Abishai and to all his servants, "My own son is trying to kill me. Doesn't this relative of Saul have even more reason to do so? Leave him alone and let him curse, for the LORD has told him to do it. And perhaps the LORD will see that I am being wronged and will bless me because of these curses today." So David and his men continued down the road, and Shimei kept pace with them on a nearby hillside, cursing and throwing stones and dirt at David (2 Samuel 16:5-13).

The commandments of the LORD are right, bringing joy to the heart. The commands of the LORD are clear, giving insight for living. Reverence for the LORD is pure, lasting forever. The laws of the LORD are true; each one is fair.

They are more desirable than gold, even the finest gold. They are sweeter than honey, even honey dripping from the comb (Psalm 19:8-10).

Your word is a lamp to guide my feet and a light for my path (Psalm 119:105).

We will talk about what David discovered later

David Saw Life as a Battle

David saw life as a battle
Even as a young boy
And he knew that this battle produced other battles
These battles, to David, were the same in one unique way
They all belonged to God
David also knew that those who had faith in God
A relationship with God
A deep and abiding relationship with God
God would see them through each and every battle

> "Don't worry about this Philistine," David told Saul. "I'll go fight him!"
>
> "Don't be ridiculous!" Saul replied. "There's no way you can fight this Philistine and possibly win! You're only a boy, and he's been a man of war since his youth."
>
> But David persisted. "I have been taking care of my father's sheep and goats," he said. "When a lion or a bear comes to steal a lamb from the flock, I go after it with a club and rescue the lamb from its mouth. If the animal turns on me, I catch it by the jaw and club it to death. I have done this to both lions and bears, and I'll do it to this pagan Philistine, too . . .

(Why?)

> "For he has defied the armies of the living God! The (same) Lord who rescued me from the claws of the lion and the bear will rescue me from this Philistine!"

Saul finally consented. "All right, go ahead," he said. "And may the lord be with you!"

Then Saul gave David his own armor—a bronze helmet and a coat of mail. David put it on, strapped the sword over it, and took a step or two to see what it was like, for he had never worn such things before.

"I can't go in these," he protested to Saul. "I'm not used to them." So David took them off again. He picked up five smooth stones from a stream and put them into his shepherd's bag. Then, armed only with his shepherd's staff and sling, he started across the valley to fight the Philistine.

Goliath walked out toward David with his shield bearer ahead of him, sneering in contempt at this ruddy-faced boy. "Am I a dog," he roared at David, "that you come at me with a stick?" And he cursed David by the names of his gods. "Come over here, and I'll give your flesh to the birds and wild animals!" Goliath yelled.

David replied to the Philistine, "You come to me with sword, spear, and javelin, but I come to you in the name of the lord of Heaven's Armies—the God of the armies of Israel, whom you have defied. Today the LORD will conquer you, and I will kill you and cut off your head. And then I will give the dead bodies of your men to the birds and wild animals, and the whole world will know that there is a God in Israel! And everyone assembled here will know that the LORD rescues his people, but not with sword and spear. This is the LORD's battle, and he will give you to us!"

As Goliath moved closer to attack, David quickly ran out to meet him. Reaching into his shepherd's bag and taking out a stone, he hurled it with his sling and hit the Philistine in the forehead. The stone sank in, and Goliath stumbled and fell face down on the ground.

So David triumphed over the Philistine with only a sling and a stone, for he had no sword. Then David ran over and pulled Goliath's sword from its sheath. David used it to kill him and cut off his head.

When the Philistines saw that their champion was dead, they turned and ran. Then the men of Israel and Judah gave a great shout of triumph and rushed after the Philistines, chasing them as far as Gath and the gates of Ekron. The bodies of the dead and wounded Philistines were strewn all along the road from Shaaraim, as far as Gath and Ekron (1 Samuel 17:32-52).

Our battles all belong to God

And He will see us through each and every battle

CHAPTER 12

Jesus, Our Model for Living effectively through the Battles

We have to understand

Jesus entered a world of conflict

Conflict in every sense of the word

Politically

Socially

As well as spiritually

There was a battle going on when Jesus arrived here on earth

As there is one going on now

And there were more battles that erupted because of Jesus

Because of His coming

Jesus' coming to Earth

We can say

Was a clash of Kingdoms
The Kingdom of Heaven
And Satan's kingdom
The devil's kingdom
The Kingdom of Darkness
Jesus
The infant Jesus
Was the Purpose and Plan of God
God's purpose and plan announced
God's promise
Way back in the Garden
When life got turned into a battle
God said (to the serpent)

> "Because you have done this, you are cursed more than all animals, domestic and wild. You will crawl on your belly, groveling in the dust as long as you live. And I will cause hostility between you and the woman, and between your offspring and her offspring. He will strike your head, and you will strike his heel" (Genesis 3:14-15).

The Birth of Jesus

When Jesus was born
When He entered the battle
The fray

When His birth was announced
Became known
It was as if, as they say, "All hell broke loose!"
It was as if all of the forces of hell were alerted
The devil anointed and appointed
And entered another of his earthly agents and tool
Herod

> About that time some wise men from eastern lands arrived in Jerusalem, asking, "Where is the newborn king of the Jews? We saw his star as it rose, and we have come to worship him."
>
> King Herod was deeply disturbed when he heard this, as was everyone in Jerusalem. He called a meeting of the leading priests and teachers of religious law and asked, "Where is the Messiah supposed to be born?"
>
> "In Bethlehem in Judea," they said, "for this is what the prophet wrote: 'And you, O Bethlehem in the land of Judah, are not least among the ruling cities of Judah, for a ruler will come from you who will be the shepherd for my people Israel.'"
>
> Then Herod called for a private meeting with the wise men, and he learned from them the time when the star first appeared. Then he told them, "Go to Bethlehem and search carefully for the child. And when you find him, come back and tell me so that I can go and worship him, too!" (Matthew 2:1-8)

> When it was time to leave, they (the wise men) returned to their own country by another route,

for God had warned them in a dream not to return to Herod.

After the wise men were gone, an angel of the Lord appeared to Joseph in a dream. "Get up! Flee to Egypt with the child and his mother," the angel said. "Stay there until I tell you to return, because Herod is going to search for the child to kill him."

That night Joseph left for Egypt with the child and Mary, his mother, and they stayed there until Herod's death. This fulfilled what the Lord had spoken through the prophet: "I called my Son out of Egypt" (Matthew 2:12-15).

The Purpose for Jesus' coming

Our main battle is a spiritual one

Jesus came to die

To die on the Cross

He came to make peace

Peace between God and humans

Jesus came to restore the kingdom

The kingdom that was lost way back in the Garden

When life was turned into a battle

The first humans sinned

They violated God's Word

The evil one

Satan

The devil

Did not cause the first humans to sin

He took advantage of their sin

He came alongside to coax and cajole

To tempt

To deceive

And to lie about God and His Word

So Satan tempted Adam and Eve

They, of their own choosing, decided to go against God's Word

From that moment

Life became a battle

A struggle

A challenge of existence

The battle that was life produced other battles

God created humans to rule

To have power and control over their environment and everything in that environment

Satan, through his deception, was also able to usurp humans' dominion power over the earth

In addition to the battle the world was thrust into, Satan now had control over what was intended for us humans to rule over

Satan "stole" the dominion power of humans in the earthly realm, where he continues his opposition to God

Satan is diametrically opposed to God

Satan hates what God loves and loves what God hates

Satan's job is to destroy the plan, program, and works of God

He does this mainly through temptation

Before God removed, because of sin, His Spirit from human beings' spirits

God's work is to destroy the works of the devil

Much of the conditions

Not all

The sicknesses

Diseases

Demon possessions

Death

And dying are the result of life being turned into a battle and the works of the devil

We say not all because we know that God ultimately is in control

There are some things that God allows to demonstrate His power

To bring glory and honor to His name

To make the world and the spirit world know and understand that He, God, is God

He is the Lord

So when Jesus entered the world, the world was wracked by conflict

Peace was non-existent

Again

Peace

Spiritual peace

Peace between God and humans
Inner
Spiritual peace
Was non-existent

The primary peace that God
Jesus
Sought was the peace between God and humans
This is why some of the first words out of Jesus's mouth were:

> Repent of your sins and turn to God, for the Kingdom of Heaven is near! (Matthew 4:17).

In other words
Make a change
Change your minds
Change your hearts
Change your life
Turn your life completely around and move in a new direction
Confess your sins and commit your life to God
Know that we are sinners
Rebels
Fighting a futile fight against God
Seek peace

Jesus said to the men He chose and called,

"Follow me, and I will make you fishers for humans"

Fishers of souls

Jesus said, in His first sermon

The Sermon on the Mount

> God blesses those who are poor and realize their need for him, for the Kingdom of Heaven is theirs. God blesses those who mourn, for they will be comforted. God blesses those who are humble, for they will inherit the whole earth. God blesses those who hunger and thirst for justice, for they will be satisfied (Matthew 5:3-6).

Jesus Saw Life as a Battle

Jesus saw all of life as a battle

A battle that, because of sin and the tempting work of the devil, was dealing a crushing blow to God's children

God's offspring

His most cherished creation

In this day and age, it needs to be said

Humans

Not animals

Are God's most cherished creation

We are God's most cherished creation

And He loves us dearly

God wants us to turn to Him so that we would have peace

Freedom

Joy

Happiness

A peace, joy, and happiness that this world cannot give because it is in the throes of the evil one

The devil

The devil does not have any control over God

Jesus

Jesus said the enemy "has no part in me!" (John 14:30)

That is to say, no power

Control

Or influence

As a matter of fact, just the opposite is true

God

Jesus

Has control over all of life

Sickness

Death

Dying

Diseases

Debilitating and crippling conditions

Blindness

Nature

Even demons and the devil

His disciples

> The disciples were amazed. "Who is this man?" they asked. "Even the winds and waves obey him!" (Matthew 8:27).

The demons

> When Jesus arrived on the other side of the lake, in the region of the Gadarenes, two men who were possessed by demons met him. They came out of the tombs and were so violent that no one could go through that area.
>
> They began screaming at him, "Why are you interfering with us, Son of God? Have you come here to torture us before God's appointed time?" (Matthew 8:28-29).

The devil's control of the world

His ability to harass and torment God's children

His people

Is only temporary

And the devil and his band of demons know it!

So Jesus came to die

The perfect sacrifice that was foreshadowed long ago in the Old Testament under the old covenant

The agreement between God and humans

It is wise to read and pay attention to what is written in the Old Testament

Moses
The Law
The prophets
And the Psalms
It all points to Jesus
The apostle Paul says:

> All Scripture is inspired by God and is useful to teach us what is true and to make us realize what is wrong in our lives. It corrects us when we are wrong and teaches us to do what is right. God uses it to prepare and equip his people to do every good work (2 Timothy 3:16-17).

Jesus was the perfect sacrifice
The Lamb of God
Sent by God to take away the sins of the world
John said what he saw from God:

> The next day John saw Jesus coming toward him and said, "Look! The Lamb of God who takes away the sin of the world! He is the one I was talking about when I said, 'A man is coming after me who is far greater than I am for he existed long before me'" (John 1:29-30).

Jesus, who knew no sin
Yet lived life as a man
Through His death on the Cross
Became the substitute for sinful humans
An atonement

And a ransom for all of humanity

A redemption

Or a cancellation of the debt that was binding

Owed

That says the wages of sin is death

The Bible says that Jesus

Who knew no sin

Became sin for us

When He took on our sins and died on the Cross

Jesus Modeled How We Are to Go Through Battles

Jesus also came to model for us how to live life successfully

How to go through the battle

And the battles

Without suffering the wounds/scars

Jesus' duel with the devil in the wilderness is a perfect example of how we are to deal with the enemy

Jesus not only knew the principles of the Word of God, but He also applied them!

> Then Jesus was led by the Spirit into the wilderness to be tempted there by the devil. For forty days and forty nights he fasted and became very hungry.
>
> During that time the devil came and said to him, "If you are the Son of God, tell these stones to become loaves of bread."

But Jesus told him, "No! The Scriptures say, 'People do not live by bread alone, but by every word that comes from the mouth of God.'"

Then the devil took him to the holy city, Jerusalem, to the highest point of the Temple, and said, "If you are the Son of God, jump off! For the Scriptures say, 'He will order his angels to protect you. And they will hold you up with their hands so you won't even hurt your foot on a stone.'"

Jesus responded, "The Scriptures also say, 'You must not test the LORD your God.'"

Next the devil took him to the peak of a very high mountain and showed him all the kingdoms of the world and their glory. "I will give it all to you," he said, "if you will kneel down and worship me."

"Get out of here, Satan," Jesus told him. "For the Scriptures say, 'You must worship the LORD your God and serve only him.'"

Then the devil went away, and angels came and took care of Jesus (Matthew 4:1-11).

Responding to the Challenges of Life

The wounds have nothing to do with what happens to us in life

The wounds—and the scars

The prolonged wounds

Have everything to do with how we respond to the battle that is life

And the battles that come from life

There are things that happen to us that we may consider wounds

No

God is saying to us that they are simply a part of the battle that is life—and the battles produced by life

They are nothing but tests and opportunities

It's all in how we respond to the tests and opportunities

We are not to respond to them in a reactive or negative manner

Allow them to make us bitter

To do so could endanger us

Cause us to sin

Lose control

Spiral out of control

Lose our grip on life

Life is not just temporal

Life is eternal

We are not to respond in kind

We are not to respond negatively

To respond is to take matters into our own hands

We are to leave everything to God

We can and should pray about them

Ask God to help us in battle

In our times of trouble

That is taking our requests and petitions into the throne room and addressing the King

To respond in kind or negatively is to incur the wounds

Wounds that can easily turn into scars

So Jesus

In His discourse on finding life

Finding peace

True and long-lasting joy and happiness as citizens of the Kingdom

Said:

> God blesses those who are persecuted for doing right, for the Kingdom of Heaven is theirs (Matthew 5:10).

Serving God

Doing His will

Sharing the good news about Jesus brings a whole new level of battle

So Jesus said:

> God blesses you when people mock you and persecute you and lie about you and say all sorts of evil things against you because you are my followers. Be happy about it! Be very glad! For a great reward awaits you in heaven. And remember, the ancient prophets were persecuted in the same way (Matthew 5:11).

Warning about the scars and the wounds that so easily turn into scars, He said:

> You have heard that our ancestors were told, 'You must not murder. If you commit murder, you are subject to judgment. But I say, if you are even angry with someone, you are subject to judgment. If you call someone an idiot, you are in danger of being brought before the court. And if you curse someone, you are in danger of the fires of hell (Matthew 5:21-22).
>
> You have heard the commandment that says, 'You must not commit adultery. But I say, anyone who even looks at a woman with lust has already committed adultery with her in his heart (Matthew 5:27-28).
>
> You have heard the law that says the punishment must match the injury: 'An eye for an eye, and a tooth for a tooth.' But I say, do not resist an evil person! If someone slaps you on the right cheek, offer the other cheek also. If you are sued in court and your shirt is taken from you, give your coat, too. If a soldier demands that you carry his gear for a mile, carry it two miles. Give to those who ask, and don't turn away from those who want to borrow (Matthew 5:38-42).

Our lives should reflect who God is

Jesus emphasized that God is love

We are to live lives that reveal the character of God

Who He is

His identity

Love

Jesus said love

True love
God's love
Agape love
Is all-encompassing
It is pure
It is forgiving

> You have heard the law that says, 'Love your neighbor' and hate your enemy. But I say, love your enemies! Pray for those who persecute you! In that way, you will be acting as true children of your Father in heaven. For he gives his sunlight to both the evil and the good, and he sends rain on the just and the unjust alike. If you love only those who love you, what reward is there for that? Even corrupt tax collectors do that much. If you are kind only to your friends, how are you different from anyone else? Even pagans do that. But you are to be perfect, even as your Father in heaven is perfect (Matthew 5:43-48).

> So if you are presenting a sacrifice at the altar in the Temple and you suddenly remember that someone has something against you, leave your sacrifice there at the altar. Go and be reconciled to that person. Then come and offer your sacrifice to God. When you are on the way to court with your adversary, settle your differences quickly. Otherwise, your accuser may hand you over to the judge, who will hand you over to an officer, and you will be thrown into prison. And if that happens, you surely won't be free again until you have paid the last penny (Matthew 5:23-26).

Forgiveness as an aspect of love
As a matter of fact

Forgiveness is love

> For this is how God loved the world: He gave his one and only Son, so that everyone who believes in him will not perish but have eternal life (John 3:16).

The apostle Paul, with the wisdom that God gave him Writes

> Love is patient and kind. Love is not jealous or boastful or proud or rude. It does not demand its own way. It is not irritable, and it keeps no record of being wronged. It does not rejoice about injustice but rejoices whenever the truth wins out. Love never gives up, never loses faith, is always hopeful, and endures through every circumstance (1 Corinthians 13:4-7).

So Jesus spoke extensively on forgiveness
Remember, forgiveness is an aspect of love
When we pray
Jesus said:

> Pray like this:
>
> Our Father in heaven, may your name be kept holy. May your Kingdom come soon. May your will be done on earth, as it is in heaven. Give us today the food we need, and forgive us our sins, as we have forgiven those who sin against us. And don't let us yield to temptation, but rescue us from the evil one.
>
> If you forgive those who sin against you, your heavenly Father will forgive you. But if you refuse to forgive others, your Father will not forgive your sins (Matthew 6:9-14).

The far-reaching implications and consequences of unforgiveness

Unforgiveness is a wound

A scar

It is a scar that resists healing

Forgiveness

On the other hand

Is a sign of healing

Love

The successful embrace of who God is

And not a rejection of God

It is faith in God

God rewards our faith and our obedience to Him

> Then Peter came to him and asked, "Lord, how often should I forgive someone who sins against me? Seven times?"
>
> "No, not seven times," Jesus replied, "but seventy times seven! Therefore, the Kingdom of Heaven can be compared to a king who decided to bring his accounts up to date with servants who had borrowed money from him. In the process, one of his debtors was brought in who owed him millions of dollars. He couldn't pay, so his master ordered that he be sold—along with his wife, his children, and everything he owned—to pay the debt.
>
> "But the man fell down before his master and begged him, 'Please, be patient with me, and I will pay it all.' Then his master was filled with pity for him, and he released him and forgave his debt.

"But when the man left the king, he went to a fellow servant who owed him a few thousand dollars. He grabbed him by the throat and demanded instant payment.

"His fellow servant fell down before him and begged for a little more time. 'Be patient with me, and I will pay it,' he pleaded. But his creditor wouldn't wait. He had the man arrested and put in prison until the debt could be paid in full.

"When some of the other servants saw this, they were very upset. They went to the king and told him everything that had happened. Then the king called in the man he had forgiven and said, 'You evil servant! I forgave you that tremendous debt because you pleaded with me. Shouldn't you have mercy on your fellow servant, just as I had mercy on you?' Then the angry king sent the man to prison to be tortured until he had paid his entire debt.

"That's what my heavenly Father will do to you if you refuse to forgive your brothers and sisters from your heart" (Matthew 8:21-35).

God does not reward our lack of faith and disobedience

As a matter of fact, when we choose to not demonstrate God's love

Remember, the love of God is to obey His commands

When we choose to not demonstrate His love

The same love He demonstrated toward us

God treats us as not one of His own

It doesn't mean that He does not love us

Or

That He abandons us
No
We abandon God
We are sinners
Some of us—sinners saved by grace
Strip away grace, and we are back to being sinners
At odds with a holy and righteous God
Condemned already
Whatever comes to us is what we deserve!

CHAPTER 13

Stories of Forgiveness and Unforgiveness

First, a personal story

Even as I was in the middle of writing this book, I realized that something was amiss in my own life

Something I needed to take care of

Attend to

I felt the weight upon me to address this interpersonal matter

I did not want to be a false prophet, so to speak

Preaching one thing while my life reflected something else

I truly believe that God has called us—those whom He has called—to live in peace

To live a life of freedom

Freedom from the wounds that can so easily turn into scars

I believe God wants us to live a life that is pure

A life of integrity

An orderly life

I am constantly reminded of the words of Jesus:

> God blesses those who are humble, for they will inherit the whole earth. God blesses those who hunger and thirst for justice, for they will be satisfied. God blesses those whose hearts are pure, for they will see God. God blesses those who work for peace, for they will be called the children of God (Matthew 5:5-9).

Jesus also said:

> "So if you are presenting a sacrifice at the altar in the Temple, and you suddenly remember that someone has something against you, leave your sacrifice there at the altar. Go and be reconciled to that person. Then come and offer your sacrifice to God" (Matthew 5:23-24).

Writing this book was like going to present my gift at the altar

I thought about my brother

I had to turn around

Reach back and attempt reconciliation

Try to make peace

Finally, Jesus remarked:

> "When you are on the way to court with your adversary, settle your differences quickly. Otherwise, your accuser may hand you over to the judge, who will hand you over to an officer, and you will be thrown into prison. And if that happens, you surely

won't be free again until you have paid the last penny" (Matthew 5:25-26).

So this dilemma I was facing

I knew it was not going to be easy

But I became so convicted I had to stop in the middle of the chapter to try to resolve the issue

The issue was that my brother and I were not on speaking terms

Something had happened and, in a fiery tone, he had told me he never wished to speak to me again

At the time, I thought he was being highly unreasonable and that I had no choice other than to oblige him

If he felt so strongly about it, what was I supposed to do, I said to myself

So we stopped speaking to each other

This went on for over two years

Then came this book that I believe God had given me to write

And the section on forgiveness

One of the things that I try to do as I read the Bible is allow it to "speak" to me and to my life and to show me any opportunity for growth, improvement

Immediately, as I started looking back over my life, the one person that loomed large in my mind, that I owed a debt to, was my brother

The Bible also says

As much as it is up to you

Make peace with all humans

Being a Doer of the Word

Like I said, I knew it was not going to be easy

How do you place that call to someone who has sworn to never speak to you again?

There is just no art to this deal

The only thing I knew I had to do was to pick up the phone and call

I had to do it

It was the right thing to do

No thinking about it

No rationalizing about it

Who did what to whom

How did it all start

I had to do it, like I said, because I was in the middle of writing about forgiveness

I couldn't just be a preacher of the Word; I had to also be a doer of the Word

Most important, however, I had to place that call to my brother—as difficult as it was—because it is what the Bible teaches:

> Never pay back evil with more evil. Do things in such a way that everyone can see you are honorable. Do all that you can to live in peace with everyone (Romans 12:17-18).

I could hear the words of Jesus:

> "So if you are presenting a sacrifice at the altar in the Temple, and you suddenly remember that someone has something against you, leave your sacrifice there at the altar. Go and be reconciled to that person. Then come and offer your sacrifice to God (Matthew 5:23-24).

So I picked up the phone

It was not easy

As difficult as it was, I felt a burden lifted

Just picking up the phone and calling

Today, my brother and I are at peace with one another

Other family members, after hearing what I had done, were also moved to mend broken-down fences of their own

I am not bragging

Why did I do it?

I did it because deep down inside, I just felt—and still do—that God wants us to live at peace

Free

He wants us to live free of the scars

Living free of the scars, I believe, is part of our wholeness, spiritual well-being

Having our lives in order

And most important, being able to worship God "in spirit and truth"—just as He intended

And I did it because I could not live a hypocritical life

As I said, I was in the middle of writing this book on how to go through the battles without the scars

I did it because, at this point in my life, I did not want to just be a knower and sharer of the Word, but also a doer of the Word!

God is Holy

Morally upright and perfect

We are not perfect creatures, but we are to strive for perfection

The Bible says that we must strive for holiness just as He is holy (1 Peter 1:16)

It also says without holiness, no one will see God (Hebrews 12:14)

Holiness means holiness

Righteous

Outstanding

Right standing

Right standing with the God who created us

At peace with God and our fellow human beings

Let me implore you

Let me beseech you

Let me plead with you

If there is some outstanding issue in your life

A disagreement

A rift

An ongoing conflict

A grievance
A grudge
Anything that you are still carrying
Holding on to
It doesn't matter whether you are wrong or right
I did not necessarily think that I was wrong in this situation
In my dispute with my brother
I just knew that it was something still "hanging out there"
We must remove the impediments in our lives and to our lives
Again, we were created to worship God
God is spirit
We must worship Him in spirit and truth
Our spirit must become one with His Spirit
For us to worship God, then, we must be spiritually cleansed
Pure
Without blemish
Of course, I am speaking in spiritual terms
For us to become one with God
Worship Him as we were created and designed to do
We must first ask God to come into our hearts and change us
Who we are
Then we must step up
Live lives worthy of our new King

We must, ourselves, lead a life that is without impediment to worship

The prayer or the words we would have spoken to God

All of this would be null and void until we repaired the relationship between us and our fellow human beings

The Story of Antwan Fisher

I don't endorse or recommend movies

I have come to learn that people have their own tastes and preferences when it comes to movies

Some people are very sensitive to the language used in movies

However, sometimes, you watch a movie—or read a book—and the story just speaks to you

It is relevant to a situation or an issue that you are dealing with

The movie Antwan Fisher is one such story

Antwan Fisher, the main character, was a deeply troubled and "wounded" young man

He had many unresolved issues in his life—from growing up

These unresolved issues turned Antwan into a social misfit

A recluse

They also made him, as the story shows, somewhat of a "menace" to society

Withdrawn

Easily angered

Moping

A real live tinderbox of a young man

Always lashing out at others—provoked or unprovoked

In the early parts of the movie it is questionable as to whether or not Antwan knows what is ailing him

Two things happen to Antwan Fisher

One, he is forced to seek help, counseling

And two, he finds love

The navy psychologist encourages Antwan to "dig deep within" himself to locate the source of his "problem"

Part of "the problem" is he had had a very troubled life stretching all the way back to his childhood

Antwan had suffered some deep wounds that had failed to heal

In short, the young naval officer was living close to the edge, right on the border, where his "wounds" had already begun to turn into real wounds/scars

The wound of anger can be a terrible thing

Anger, that is repressed anger, can be explosive

Able to explode at any time

At the drop of a hat, as we say

Our "wounds" can be something that happened a long time ago

Many years ago

Stretching all the way back to childhood

We can be walking around with what we perceive as wounds that have just not healed

Antwan lived in a rough neighborhood

At a young, tender age of about four, Antwan saw his father gunned down right in front of his eyes

As a teenager, he saw his best friend's life also taken tragically and senselessly by gun violence

To compound these pains, he had to go and live in a foster home

There, he was abused physically, emotionally, and sexually by people who were supposed to be caring for him

This was the nature of Antwan's life

His battle

The battles that Antwan experienced in life really hurt him

They made him bitter

Angry

Resentful

Full of rage

And irritable

Antwan Fisher became deeply wounded

Living with a wound that had progressed into a scar

These were wounds that had crept in

Wounds that he had allowed to grow

To sit and fester in his life

The wounds had turned into scars

He carried with him the pain and the anguish of those wounds into his adult life

The scars had settled in

He was on that slippery slope

He was teetering

He was right on the verge of self-destructing when he met his first real "father" figure

The navy's chief psychologist helped Antwan on the road to recovery

Helped him see that part of his struggle

That part of the young man's life he, the naval psychologist, felt was his greatest missing piece and dilemma

The part of his life that was missing

A connection—a real connection—to family—His own family

The psychologist posed this as a most necessary step for Antwan

A badly needed journey

The journey that would potentially bring healing to Antwan's troubled life

The story of Antwan Fisher is indeed a story about finding healing

Tragically, however, it is a story about how we cannot find that healing in and of ourselves

When we decide to go it alone in life

Leave no room for God

Recognize the essential need for God

We always make a mess out of things

We have already established that only God can heal us of our wounds

We cannot heal ourselves

Others cannot heal us

Time does not heal our wounds

Only God can

And at the end of the movie, Antwan cuts a tragic and pitiable figure as he stands in the doorway railing at his mom—a deeply troubled and wounded woman herself—about abandoning and not loving him

At the old foster home, Antwan confronted the people who had tortured his life, abused—physically, emotionally, psychologically, and sexually

Those he felt had wounded him in the worst way

Who had helped to "cripple" him mentally and psychologically

"Look at me! Look at me!"

"You thought you could break me!"

"You thought you could destroy me! But look at me; I am still standing! I am still standing!"

"You can't destroy me!"

Did Antwan find solace for his "wounds"?

Did he arrive at peace?

The movie, Antwan Fisher, reminds us that true peace can only come from God

Another Story That Stands Out

On a trip back home to the Bahamas, we visited one of the lesser developed "family islands"

It reminded me of the rural South

Plain-speaking, honest people

People who told you exactly what they thought and how they felt

I was with a group of ministers and business people

We stopped to give a young lady a ride

Under the weight of her luggage, she just looked like she was struggling, having a difficult time

Turned out she was very talkative

She was very forthcoming with the hardships she was experiencing on the island

Apparently, she had just moved back home to her native island from the main island

She wanted to build a home for herself and the family she was planning on having

However, life was tough

Not everyone was willing to help her realize her dream

She had an aunt who she had asked to cede to her a small plot on the family plot to build her future home

Her aunt had said no

Feeling wounded and hurt by this, she said:

"But you know what?

That's okay

I can't wait for her to die!

And when she does, I am going to go and find the biggest rock I can find and throw it on her grave!"

What can you say?

Life is a battle

For the rich and the poor

For everyone

CHAPTER 14

The Absolute Key to Life

(How not to be affected by the battles!)

So Jesus taught that what matters most in life is to have a relationship with God

This is the most essential relationship in all of life

We are also supposed to love our fellow human beings

In a relationship with God, we are to live a life worthy of God

Worthy of our calling

Reflecting His character

His identity

Who He is

Because we don't choose God

God chooses us

A relationship with God was made possible by God

It's His grace

Unmerited

Undeserved favor that He has granted

And grants

To sinful humanity

It involves no work

No rituals

No duties

No works

We are saved

Granted a relationship with God when we believe in the One He has sent

His one and only begotten Son

Jesus Christ

Our Most Essential Relationship

A relationship with God is critical

Crucial

Essential to life

No matter what happens to us in this life, when we have a relationship with God, it is as if we are covered

We are covered!

We are covered by the blood of Jesus Christ

The Bible says

When I see the blood, I will pass over you (Exodus 12:13)
We are covered for all eternity
We may die physically
But physical death and dying is not all there is to life
Our lives extend beyond the grave
Beyond us breathing our last breath
Jesus said in Matthew 9:24:

> "The girl isn't dead; she's only asleep."

Jesus also said:

> "I am the resurrection and the life. Anyone who believes in me will live, even after dying. Everyone who lives in me and believes in me will never ever die" (John 11:25-26).

There is this "little" incident that the apostle Luke recorded

We say "little" because the import of it can be easily missed
It is about the ultimate tragedy in life

> About this time Jesus was informed that Pilate had murdered some people from Galilee as they were offering sacrifices at the Temple. "Do you think those Galileans were worse sinners than all the other people from Galilee?" Jesus asked. "Is that why they suffered? Not at all! And you will perish, too, unless you repent of your sins and turn to God. And what about the eighteen people who died when the tower

in Siloam fell on them? Were they the worst sinners in Jerusalem? No, and I tell you again that unless you repent, you will perish, too" (Luke 13:1-5).

Jesus wanted His disciples to know that the ultimate tragedy in life is not death

Dying

But the greatest tragedy is a life without God

Again, in our relationship with God, we are to live a life worthy of Him

Again, God is love

Love is pure

It knows no hate

It is not diluted

Mixed

Tinged with hate or jealousy or envy or prejudice that leads to discrimination

God's love is an unadulterated, unconditional love

It is a love that is kind

Compassionate

Generous

That gives

And that is always giving

It doesn't react to anything

What the person's race is

Their gender

Their nationality

Their religion

Whether they are rich or poor

Immigrant or citizen

Love just loves

Reflecting God

The story of the Good Samaritan is perhaps one of the most telling and revealing stories that Jesus told to capture the nature of God

The essence of who God is

How the story begins is also important

> One day an expert in religious law stood up to test Jesus by asking him this question: "Teacher, what should I do to inherit eternal life?"
>
> Jesus replied, "What does the law of Moses say? How do you read it?"
>
> The man answered, "'You must love the LORD your God with all your heart, all your soul, all your strength, and all your mind.' And 'Love your neighbor as yourself.'"
>
> "Right!" Jesus told him. "Do this and you will live!"
>
> The man wanted to justify his actions, so he asked Jesus, "And who is my neighbor?"
>
> Jesus replied with a story: "A Jewish man was traveling from Jerusalem down to Jericho, and he was attacked

by bandits. They stripped him of his clothes, beat him up, and left him half dead beside the road.

"By chance a priest came along. But when he saw the man lying there, he crossed to the other side of the road and passed him by. A Temple assistant walked over and looked at him lying there, but he also passed by on the other side.

"Then a despised Samaritan came along, and when he saw the man, he felt compassion for him. Going over to him, the Samaritan soothed his wounds with olive oil and wine and bandaged them. Then he put the man on his own donkey and took him to an inn, where he took care of him. The next day he handed the innkeeper two silver coins, telling him, 'Take care of this man. If his bill runs higher than this, I'll pay you the next time I'm here.'

"Now which of these three would you say was a neighbor to the man who was attacked by bandits?" Jesus asked.

The man replied, "The one who showed him mercy."

Then Jesus said, "Yes, now go and do the same" (Luke 10:25-37).

Jesus also taught that the key to a deep and abiding relationship with Him is the Word of God

The Bible is the Word of God

Not just knowing it

It is not just for reading

Studying

Meditating on scriptures

Even though meditating on the Word of God is a good idea

The Bible is not meant to just stay on some bookshelf
It is meant for reading, hearing, and doing
You see, the Word of God
All of Jesus' commands, His promises, His teachings
The words He spoke are principles
Principles are deep and profound fundamental truths
Laws
Like the law of gravity
To be obeyed
Principles are meant to preserve us
Prosper us
Keep us safe
This is what David discovered about God's Word

So Jesus said in Matthew:

> "Anyone who listens to my teaching and follows it is wise, like a person who builds a house on solid rock. Though the rain comes in torrents and the floodwaters rise and the winds beat against that house, it won't collapse because it is built on bedrock. But anyone who hears my teaching and doesn't obey it is foolish, like a person who builds a house on sand. When the rains and floods come and the winds beat against that house, it will collapse with a mighty crash!" (Matthew 7:24-27).

Storm is just another word for battle
Life is a battle

As a battle, life produces other battles

The battles can be intense

But no matter the intensity of the storm

As long as we have the Word of God buried deep in our hearts

As long as we are "standing on the Word"

Obeying the Word

Doing what it says

It doesn't matter the ferocity and the sound of the wind

The swell and the height of the waves

Our lives are secure

God Offers Peace in Our Battles

Jesus is the Peace of God

Jesus came to set us free

Jesus came to give us life

We have life

A physical form of life

But Jesus came to give us life

And life more abundantly

A spiritual life that is to be lived in the presence of God forever

Jesus said:

My peace I give[3]

---

[3] John 14:27

Whom the Son sets free is free indeed[4]

Come to me all who are heavy-laden and I will give you rest[5]

Rest from our burdens

Rest from our loads

Rest from our battles

Rest and healing for our wounds

God's presence and His power in us allow us to live life successfully

Triumphantly

God's presence and His power allow us to go through the battles without experiencing the scars

The Bible is clear on the powerful presence of God in our lives

In the book of Genesis, the story of Joseph, it says

Time and time again

The Lord was with Joseph!

> The LORD was with Joseph, so he succeeded in everything he did as he served in the home of his Egyptian master (Genesis 39:2).
>
> But the LORD was with Joseph in the prison and showed him his faithful love. And the LORD made Joseph a favorite with the prison warden. Before long, the warden put Joseph in charge of all the other prisoners and over everything that happened in the

---

[4] John 8:36
[5] Matthew 11:28

> prison. The warden had no more worries, because Joseph took care of everything (Genesis 39:21-23).

The LORD was with him and caused everything he did to succeed

God Goes With Us into Battles

As David said—and as Joseph's life demonstrated—God can and does prepare a table before us in the presence of our enemies

Praise be unto the eternal God, who is the same

Yesterday

Today

And forever![6]

Not only does God go into battles with us, but he also miraculously bandages up our wounds

Makes our paths smooth

And—again, miraculously—absorbs the pains, the hurts, the injustices, and the abuse

This is what it meant

> Joseph named his older son Manasseh, for he said, "God has made me forget all my troubles and everyone in my father's family." Joseph named his second son Ephraim, for he said, "God has made me fruitful in this land of my grief" (Genesis 41:51-52).

---

[6] Hebrews 13:8

God does not spare us the battles
But God can and does go with us through the battles
It is all God
The battle—and the battles—all belong to Him
He is in control
Let Him control things
We will more than likely make a mess of things
As life and history have shown, we have a propensity to

Our approach to life should be the same as Joseph
We should move ourselves out of the way
Not taking action to right our wrongs or take revenge
Remember
Love
Forgive
Let God take care of the rest
This is how we go through the battles without the scars

God Is Sovereign over Our Lives

We need to understand that God is involved in every step of our lives

He orders our steps

He plans and orchestrates—if we will let Him—our journey, our battle, and our battles for His and our glory

We need to understand this

We need to become as acutely aware of this as Joseph was

> "Please, come closer," he said to them. So they came closer. And he said again, "I am Joseph, your brother, whom you sold into slavery in Egypt. But don't be upset, and don't be angry with yourselves for selling me to this place. It was God who sent me here ahead of you to preserve your lives. This famine that has ravaged the land for two years will last five more years, and there will be neither plowing nor harvesting. God has sent me ahead of you to keep you and your families alive and to preserve many survivors. So it was God who sent me here, not you! And he is the one who made me an adviser to Pharaoh—the manager of his entire palace and the governor of all Egypt (Genesis 45:4-8).

Again

> But now that their father was dead, Joseph's brothers became fearful. "Now Joseph will show his anger and pay us back for all the wrong we did to him," they said.
>
> So they sent this message to Joseph: "Before your father died, he instructed us to say to you: 'Please forgive your brothers for the great wrong they did to you—for their sin in treating you so cruelly.' So we, the servants of the God of your father, beg you to forgive our sin." When Joseph received the message, he broke down and wept. Then his brothers came and threw themselves down before Joseph. "Look, we are your slaves!" they said.
>
> But Joseph replied, "Don't be afraid of me. Am I God, that I can punish you? You intended to harm me, but God intended it all for good. He brought me to this position so I could save the lives of many people. No, don't be afraid. I will continue to take care of you

and your children." So he reassured them by speaking kindly to them (Genesis 50:15-21).

Joseph is the quintessentially human example of how we can, ourselves, go through the battles without the scars

We might be tempted to say

Ah well, I can understand Jesus going successfully through the battles

Avoiding the scars

He was and is God

It is tempting for us to think this way

Even though the Bible says that Jesus was also fully human

> So then, since we have a great High Priest who has entered heaven, Jesus the Son of God, let us hold firmly to what we believe. This High Priest of ours understands our weaknesses, for he faced all of the same tastings we do, yet he did not sin (Hebrews 4:14-15).

However, Joseph is yet another example

Joseph's brothers said:

> Speaking among themselves, they said, "Clearly we are being punished because of what we did to Joseph long ago. **We saw his anguish when he pleaded for his life**, but we wouldn't listen. That's why we're in this trouble" (Genesis 42:21, emphasis mine).

God loved Joseph

God chose Joseph

Joseph did not choose God

Joseph responded to God's love—being chosen—with a show of his love for God

Like those of us who have been chosen by God when we accepted His Grace, Joseph believed God

He surrendered

He put his faith and trust in God

He committed his life to God

Joseph became completely committed to God and His Word

In other words, Joseph did exactly what Jesus instructs us to do

He not only "heard" the Word but "did" the Word

Joseph built his entire life upon the Word of God

Jesus!

As a result, Joseph was able to go through the battles without the scars

Jesus, Our Perfect Model and Guide

In the book of Isaiah, we find these words:

> He was oppressed and treated harshly, yet he never said a word. He was led like a lamb to the slaughter. And as a sheep is silent before the shearers, he did not open his mouth (Isaiah 53:7).

All of Isaiah chapter 53

Talks about Jesus' life

His battle

And some of the battles he went through

The wounds he experienced or suffered

What is interesting, however, is that the wounds Jesus suffered were not His own

They were not produced in Him

He didn't internalize them

He was not responsible for the wounds He suffered

It says in Isaiah 53:3-5:

> He was despised and rejected—a man of sorrows, acquainted with deepest grief. We turned our backs on him and looked the other way. He was despised, and we did not care.
>
> Yet it was our weaknesses he carried; it was our sorrows that weighed him down. And we thought his troubles were a punishment from God, a punishment for his own sins! But he was pierced for our rebellion, crushed for our sins (emphasis mine).

He was beaten so we could be whole

He was whipped so we could be healed

This means that all of the wounds

The sins added to his weight

His burden

His battle

In effect, what Isaiah saw was Jesus carrying the weight of all our sins

The sins of the entire world

All of the wounds that we had produced on the inside of us

Sins like anger

Hatred

Rage

Bitterness

Resentment

Jealousy

Revenge

And the desire for revenge

Unforgiveness

And the spirit of unforgiveness

Covetousness or greed

Pride or a lack of humility

And a host of other wounds

Many of which had turned into scars

Hardened wounds

Manifested wounds

Murder

Adultery

Sexual perversions

And so forth

Indeed, the weight of all the sins of the world

None of them belonging to Him
However, they bore Him down
Added to His battle
His life
Again it says:

> Yet it was our weaknesses he carried; it was our sorrows that weighed him down.

He was beaten so we could be whole

He was whipped so we could be healed

We see this grief

We sense the weight that bore Jesus down

Jesus' battle the night of His arrest in the Garden of Gethsemane

Matthew writes:

> He walked away, about a stone's throw, and knelt down and prayed, "Father, if you are willing, please take this cup of suffering away from me. Yet I want your will to be done, not mine." Then an angel from heaven appeared and strengthened him. He prayed more fervently, and he was in such agony of spirit that his sweat fell to the ground like great drops of blood.

First of all, the angel coming down from heaven to strengthen Him reminds us of what the apostle Paul said:

> The temptations in your life are no different from what others experience. And God is faithful. He will not allow the temptation to be more than you can

> stand. When you are tempted, he will show you a way out so that you can endure (1 Corinthians 10:13).

Secondly, we see Jesus in His full humanity

He is praying to God, the Father

Under the strain and facing death, like any of us would be, He is conflicted

In Jesus' mind there is a battle going on

He knows what is confronting Him

His impending death

And all of the pain

Hurt

And humiliation that entails

So He prays to the Father

In earnest prayer

And He says:

Father

Is there another way to do this?

> If you are willing, please take this cup of suffering away from me.

Death and dying

Just the thought of it alone

Presents its own set of challenges

Jesus' knowledge of what form His death would take

The extreme cruelty that was Roman crucifixion must have also weighed on Jesus

Earlier, He had spoken to His disciples about it several times:

> "The Son of Man must suffer many terrible things," he said. "He will be rejected by the elders, the leading priests, and the teachers of religious law. He will be killed, but on the third day he will be raised from the dead" (Luke 9:22).

Let us step back for a moment

Understand why Jesus came to earth

Jesus came to die

He came to die as a sacrifice for all of humanity

However, Jesus, in coming, revealed to us God

Who God is

His character

His identity

In revealing God to us

Jesus also modeled for us God's ways

God's way of doing things

How God would have us act

Behave

Think

And what He would have us say

It is important to note, also, that in coming to earth, Jesus had submitted Himself to God

He was submitted and committed to God

First of all, Jesus modeled what it means to be submitted and committed all at the same time

He said

"Father, if you are willing, please take this cup of suffering away from me"

But then He said something else

Something important

Something we can all learn from

He said

"Yet I want your will to be done, not mine."

Hallelujah!

In His darkest hour

At what must have been the height of His struggle

His battle

When the battle was so intense

That his sweat fell to the ground like great drops of blood

Jesus submitted His will to God's will

As difficult as this moment was

Jesus said

I want your will to be done

He said

Your will be done!

Your will

Not mine

The lesson here is that no matter what we are going through in life
No matter how intense the battle
There is a right way and a wrong way
Let us lean not to our own understanding
Let us not succumb to our own emotions and desires
Let us be so committed to God
That we put His Word
His commandments
First
Let us accede
Accede to His will

We live our lives at the intersection of our battles and our wounds
God said to Cain:
Just do the "right" thing
Adam and Eve knew what that "right" thing was
They chose to go with what they saw looked attractive
Pleasant to the eye
Good to eat
Adam and Eve knew God's Word
God's will for their lives
But they chose their own way
Jesus modeled what should take precedence in our lives over everything

We are talking about how to go through the battles without the scars

In addition

Isaiah said:

> He was oppressed and treated harshly, yet he never said a word. He was led like a lamb to the slaughter. And as a sheep is silent before the shearers, he did not open his mouth (Isaiah 53:7).

What is Isaiah saying?

Jesus

Completely innocent

He was treated harshly

He was oppressed **and** treated harshly

Some of us

We don't have to be oppressed

We could just think we are oppressed

And we will open our mouths

Jesus

Our perfect model

Never said a word!

He was led like a lamb to the slaughter

Like a sheep is silent before the shearer

He did not open His mouth

He didn't have anything to say

Which means He did not express any

Anger

Bitterness

Resentment

Hatred

Jesus didn't plead His case

Curse at them

He said nothing—bad or good

He did not open His mouth

He said nothing!

Jesus also modeled for us how we are to practice what we preach

Then, on the Cross

Just before dying

Before He gasped His last breath

Jesus prayed for forgiveness for His enemies

> Jesus said, "Father, forgive them, for they don't know what they are doing" (Luke 23:34).

Forgiveness

We said

Forgiveness is an aspect of love

This would mean that Jesus, up and till the very end, showed love for His enemies

Jesus also trusted God

He knew that God would take care of Him

Finally

We said that going through the battle without the scars

Leads to our success

Our victory

Our triumph

And our promotion

John said:

> A jar of sour wine was sitting there, so they soaked a sponge in it, put it on a hyssop branch, and held it up to his lips. When Jesus had tasted it, he said, "It is finished!" Then he bowed his head and gave up his spirit (John 19:29-30).
>
> Jesus prayed:
>
> "Father, the hour has come. Glorify your Son so he can give glory back to you" (John 17:1-2).

And finally:

> Though he was God, he did not think of equality with God as something to cling to. Instead, he gave up his divine privileges; he took the humble position of a slave and was born as a human being. When he appeared in human form, he humbled himself in obedience to God and died a criminal's death on a cross. Therefore, God elevated him to the place of highest honor and gave him the name above all other names, that at the name of Jesus every knee should bow, in heaven and on earth and under the earth, and every tongue declare that Jesus Christ is Lord, to the glory of God the Father! (Philippians 2:6-11).

Finally

Life is a battle

As a battle, it produces, manufactures, and spawns other battles

Battles produce wounds

However, our wounds do not have to turn into scars!

Life was meant to be lived with and in humility

Humbled before God

Surrendered to His will

In a deep and abiding relationship with God

Obedient to His Word

Doing what His Word says

Trusting God

Not trusting ourselves

Not relying on our own strength

Not living life reactively

Not taking offenses

But allowing God's Power

His Holy Spirit

To lead, guide, and direct us at all times

Only then can we go through the battle—and the battles—without the scars

About the Author

Bertram Smith is an author, educator, speaker, and poet who shares his love for the culture, beauty, and history of his birthplace, The Bahamas. He is the author of the poetry collection From the Puddle to the Pond (2020) and the middle-grade adventure fiction novella The Blue Hole (2021). He is currently working on a follow-up to From the Puddle to the Pond, as well as several other books to encourage others who are walking through difficult times in their lives.

With an extensive background teaching in public school, colleges, and university settings and active in church ministries over the many years, Bertram also enjoys reading, writing, cooking, fishing, and spending time with his family. He is the proud father of two beautiful daughters, Falashade and Jamani. Bertram lives with his beautiful, darling wife, Leslie, in Atlanta, Georgia.

You can connect with Bertram on Facebook on the page "Books to Inspire Us."

About the Illustrator

Patrick Noze was born in Haiti in the province of Jeremie, 'City of Poets.' He is a third-generation sculptor and painter. "I am always thinking about the wonders of the world from its simplest to its most complex shapes. To my eyes, the world is a large canvas. Everything I see, dream, or encounter, I use as an inspiration for my work." He attended Pratt Institute, School of Art and Science. He is presently very involved in his community and serves on a voluntary basis on the Advisory Council for Art in Cultural Affairs. He lives in Orange County, Florida, with his family. Find out more at patricknoze.com.

www.ingramcontent.com/pod-product-compliance
Lightning Source LLC
LaVergne TN
LVHW010310070526
838199LV00065B/5508